Eugenio Barba
and the Golden Apple

Eugenio Barba and the Golden Apple

Witnessing Odin Teatret's Rehearsals

Foreword by Eugenio Barba

DIANA COZMA

THE CHOIR PRESS

Copyright © 2021 Diana Cozma

All rights reserved. No part of this publication may be reproduced or transmitted in any form or by any means, electronic or mechanical including photocopying, recording or any information storage or retrieval system, without prior permission in writing from the publishers.

The right of Diana Cozma to be identified as the author of this work has been asserted by her in accordance with the Copyright, Designs and Patents Act 1988

First published in the United Kingdom in 2021 by
The Choir Press

ISBN 978-1-78963-204-0

Foreword by Eugenio Barba
Cover design: Ovidiu Petca
Eugenio Barba, Holstebro, September 2016, photograph by Francesco Galli

Diana Cozma (5 December 1962, Cluj-Napoca, Romania) is an actress, writer, translator, member of the Writers' Union of Romania, Ph.D. associate professor habil. at the Faculty of Theatre and Film, Babeș-Bolyai University of Cluj-Napoca. Her previous books in Romanian include *Leave Your Boots and Get Out!* (dramatic monologues); *The Ephemeral Dance of the Actor's Scenic Actions; Love of Violets* (short stories); *Eugenio Barba and the Golden Apple*; *The Enchained Theatre: An Essay on Jerzy Grotowski's Theatre*; *Homo Felix Experiment: A Study of Shakespeare*; *The Practitioner-Playwright*.

To Eugenio Barba and his actors

Contents

Prefazione di Eugenio Barba	x
Foreword by Eugenio Barba	xi
The biography of a dramaturgical language	1
The golden apple	2
The director-playwright	11
Quick reflections	30
Performances dreamed with eyes wide open	33
Youth without age and life without death	38
The dramaturgy of a spectator	41
Is the spectator the key?	42
Eyewitnessing	50
Imagine our Father	99
Welcome home!	107
The dance of eros-thanatos	113
Sensations-in-words	117
Face to face	124
In the storeroom	129
The physical-vocal island	131
The time to be humble	135
The training of self-becoming	138
Epistle to Augusto Omolú	141
To speak about freedom is always a must	142
The miracle of longevity	147
Azure	151
Bibliography	153

Eugenio Barba

A DIANA, UNA SCRITTRICE CHE NON DISPERÒ MAI

Il mio pensiero rievoca circostanze e dettagli, mette a fuoco volti e sguardi sfigurati dal tempo, riascolta parole e canti che mi accompagnarono quotidianamente per mesi e mesi. Un frammento del mio passato è steso davanti a me in un fiume di parole, un centinaio di pagine, come un tappeto volante.

Mi riconosco in quello che è scritto? Erano queste le mie intenzioni, i motivi che ignoravo io stesso, le conseguenze delle mie decisioni e dei miei atti? Sono giusti i commenti e le considerazioni? La mia vanità è soddisfatta per il ritratto che ne viene fuori? Troppa ammirazione nuoce.

I fatti sono corretti, mi appartengono, ogni parola constata un dato avvenuto e al contempo protegge l'essenziale. Lo occulta sapientemente dietro uno stile che resiste per trattenere la forza emotiva ed intellettuale che lo scuote.

Percepisco l'intensità dell'autrice di questo libro nel descrivere atti e pensieri del regista e degli attori che per anni l'hanno accompagnata nella sua scrittura in rumeno e inglese. Riconosco la stessa tensione, lo stesso desiderio e sforzo che sgorgano da una reazione appassionata particolare nell'essere umano: la gratitudine verso la persona che ha aperto i nostri occhi e ha svegliato le nostre energie.

Riconosco l'origine di questa scrittura, la natura del suo stile particolare. Ricorda la mia lotta con le parole o con l'incandescenza degli attori nel tentativo di sconfinare in quella dimensione della realtà che costringe ad andare aldilà di quello che siamo. È una lotta che è costantemente accompagnata dalla tentazione di desistere e abbandonare.

Lo stile è la radiografia luminosa del buio dentro di noi.

Eugenio Barba

TO DIANA, A WRITER WHO NEVER DESPAIRED

In my mind I recall circumstances and details, focus on faces and looks disfigured by time, listen to words and songs that daily accompanied me for months on end. A fragment of my past is spread out in front of me in a stream of words, about a hundred pages, like a flying carpet.

Do I recognise myself in what is written? Were these my intentions, the motives I myself ignored, the consequences of my decisions and acts? Are the comments and considerations accurate? Is my vanity satisfied with the portrait that emerges? Too much admiration is harmful.

The facts are correct, they belong to me. Each word confirms a fact that has occurred and at the same time protects the essential, cleverly concealing it behind a style that struggles to hold back the emotional and intellectual force that shakes it.

I feel the author's intensity in describing the actions and thoughts of the director and the actors who for years have accompanied her in her writing both in Romanian and English. I recognise the same tension, the same desire and effort that flow from a certain passionate reaction in the human being: gratitude towards the person who opened our eyes and awakened our energies.

I recognise the origin of this writing, the nature of its particular style. It reminds me of my struggle with words or with the incandescence of the actors, in the attempt to cross over into that dimension of reality which forces us to go beyond what we are. It is a struggle that is constantly accompanied by the temptation to abandon and give up.

Style is the luminous radiography of the darkness within us.

For many years now Eugenio Barba has been a major and constant influence on my life in the theatre. I am extremely grateful to him and his actors for allowing me the privilege of watching the rehearsals of *The Chronic Life* in Holstebro, Denmark, in September-October 2010 and February-March 2011, when I lived at Odin Teatret's guest house.

I would like to thank the wonderful people of Odin Teatret, Kai Bredholt, Thomas Bredsdorff, Roberta Carreri, Claudio Coloberti, Chiara Crupi, Jan Ferslev, Elena Floris, Lene Højmark, Nathalie Jabalé, Raúl Iaiza, Donald Kitt, Tage Larsen, Else Marie Laukvik, Sofia Monsalve, Iben Nagel Rasmussen, Antonella Diana, Pierangelo Pompa, Sigrid Post, Fausto Pro, Francesca Romana Rietti, Anne Savage, Mirella Schino, Rina Skeel, Ulrik Skeel, Nando Taviani, Valentina Tibaldi, Julia Varley, Frans Winther, Ana Woolf, for their friendship and support.

This book is a personal account of what I watched, heard and thought.

The biography of a dramaturgical language

The golden apple

I would like to believe that Eugenio Barba's road is the one on which he encounters the tree with a golden apple hanging from the highest branch and, in full daylight, without caring about the people around him, he climbs the tree and picks the apple. The fortunate apple of fate. Courage, perseverance, unshakable belief in his inner voice, which incessantly whispers to him the road he should follow, since it is his road.

Eugenio Barba, master, director, writer, visionary, is one of the world theatre reformers. Through his dramaturgy, reflections on the sense and condition of theatre art and artist, through the theatre laboratory research and rigorous studies within the sessions of the International School of Theatre Anthropology, he forges a *unifying artistic act* based on the co-existence of opposites, *simultaneities*, temporal and spatial combinations, links between past and future, East and West, producing "a Copernican revolution without which the science of the theatre at the end of the twentieth century would be incomprehensible" (Savarese 2010: 560). Barba transmits his knowledge, the results of his multi-disciplinary and trans-disciplinary research, in various forms: performances, books, workshops, seminars, conferences. Incarnating, in the *bios-in-life*, that is in the *Performance with a capital P*, a journey towards the origins of theatre, to its roots, singing and dancing, the director, after many years of crucial experiences, re-evaluates dramaturgy defining it *according to its etymology*, drama-ergon, *the work of the actions* (Barba 2010a: 8), noticing that, actually, dramaturgy has little to do with a pre-existing written text. In this regard, Craig's vision is sublimely embodied in Barba's dramaturgy as *thoughts-in-action* (Barba-Savarese 2006: 104) are revealed to the spectator's eyes: "Let me repeat again that it is not only the writer whose work is useless in the theatre. It is the musician's work which is useless there, and it is the painter's work which is useless there. All three are utterly useless. Let them keep to their preserves, let them keep to their kingdoms, and let those of the theatre return to theirs. Only when these last are once more reunited will there spring so great an art, and one so universally beloved, that I prophesy that a new religion will be found contained in it. That religion will preach no more, but it will reveal. It will not show us the definite images which the sculptor and the painter show. It will unveil thought to our eyes, silently – by movements – in visions" (Craig 1957: 123).

The director's research is reflected in his work with the actor, in his choice of the narrative sources by which he tells *not a single story, but many stories at the same time*, in the paradoxical thinking, in the detailed investigations on the nature and condition of the spectator. His dramaturgy is conceived to address simultaneously to the spectator's reptilian brain, which corresponds to *the stream of movement*, to the paleo-mammalian brain corresponding to *the stream of feeling* and to the neo-mammalian brain, that is to *the stream of thought* (Turner 1988: 161-162). Through his dramaturgy, a living organism, structured on three main levels of organisation, the director aims to provoke mental, emotional and sensorial reactions in the spectator. Like Artaud, he aspires to whip the spectator's senses, and like Brecht, to awaken his consciousness. Barba *wants his performance to inflame the memory of the spectators and caress a wound in that part within them which lives in exile. The spectator has the right to be cradled by the thousand subterfuges of entertainment, by the pleasure of the senses and the stimulation of the intellect, by emotional immediateness and aesthetic refinement. But the main point is the transfiguration of the ephemeral performance into a virus, which takes root in him, provoking a particular way of seeing: an upside-down look, one which is addressed towards the interior* (Barba 2010a: 185).

"My country can be defined as a voluntary exile. The country in which I dwell is the theatre." (Barba 2005: 1) The Country of Theatre, wherein Eugenio Barba travels tirelessly, is that of both inner and outer fascinating landscapes. I see in his voluntary exile, that of the *artist who stubbornly does not adapt to the social and political circumstances in which he lives* (Jung) and, thus, becomes capable of giving birth to a *work of living art* (Appia). His singularity also originates in his separation from the institutionalised and avant-garde theatres. His personal approach of theatre leads him to identify the existence of what he calls *The Third Theatre*. Cutting the umbilical cord from the forefathers' ways of thinking and making theatre, he succeeds in creating his own theatre, which has always been his *home*, his outstanding performances and his unique and remarkable style.

The Country of Theatre has no borders. It is the country where Eugenio Barba's road springs from Brindisi, his birthplace, weaves to Gallipoli, the home of his childhood, "an islet connected to the mainland and the suburbs by a long, windy bridge" (Barba 2010a: 5), goes to Naples, the place of his military college years where "he lives in two separate realities, simultaneously respecting the rules of each of them: the life of daily circumstances and that of an inner reality made up of daydreams and fantasies" (Barba 2010a: 51-52). It climbs tumultuously to the Northern fjords, and in Norway, he *lives out his immigrant condition* initiating into the *art of welding* (Barba 2010a: 95). Dreaming of visiting Ramakrishna's house in Calcutta, he does not think twice to embark as a sailor and travel to Asia. He attends French and Norwegian literature and history of religions courses at the University of Oslo, travels through Israel where he feels intensely the helplessness and suffering of the fragile human being *crushed by the ferocity of history* (Barba 1999a: 15). His next destination is Warsaw and then Opole at Teatr 13 Rzędów.

"Poland is my professional homeland. I always thought so because it was here I lived the fundamental years of my apprenticeship. Here I assimilated the working language, the critical attitude towards historiography, the foundations of the know-how and of the ideal tensions in the scenic craft." (Barba 2003: 1)

In *Land of Ashes and Diamonds: My Apprenticeship in Poland* followed by *26 Letters from Jerzy Grotowski to Eugenio Barba* – autobiography, reflections on theatre, story of two beautiful rebels who, with bare hands, start a war with social, political and cultural prejudices choosing theatre as their battlefield – Barba recalls the first years of his searches. It is the story of *nameless young men* who make their own way, revolutionise the theatre and become famous. A love story between master and disciple. What do they tell us? Crush the obvious under your feet. Do not obey the norm. The quest for the essence of theatre does not end with the last rehearsal for a performance. The action takes place in

Ubu's kingdom, a bleak Poland, swarming with secret police agents, informers, a land governed by political and cultural censorship. Time: 1961-1964, charmingly and humorously evoked by Barba, are his apprenticeship years spent with Grotowski at Teatr-Laboratorium 13 Rzędów in Opole. The dynamic, captivating rhythm links meaningful slices of life together. 26 letters from Jerzy Grotowski to Eugenio Barba, which unveil their friendship and lifetime collaboration, are published for the first time. It is the story of those who never give up on their dreams. Recognising their masters, they become masters themselves: "I recognise in Jerzy Grotowski my Master. Nevertheless I don't feel like his pupil and follower. His questions have become my questions. Yet my answers are becoming more and more different from his answers" (Barba 2003: 2). It is an exemplary, unique autobiography which takes the reader's breath away. And at the same time it is an account which apparently unmasks what is concealed behind the surface of things, explaining for the thousandth time that even in theatre the purpose of the mask is to finally be removed.

Eugenio Barba's writing, marked by a subtle blend of wit and charm, irony and humour, enchants the reader who allows himself/herself to be carried along within the vivid scenes that he evokes from his years in Opole. The book reveals Barba's wisdom, enthusiasm, knowledge, hunger for the essence of theatre, curiosity, fight against injustice and tremendous work.

The images of Andrzej Wajda's film, *Ashes and Diamonds*, the reading of the extraordinary texts written by Brandes and Rózewicz, by Strikowski, Andrzejewski and Tuwim, published in the issue dedicated to Poland of the periodical *Les Temps Modernes*, edited by Jean-Paul Sartre, (Nagel Rasmussen 2018: 21-22), speak to Barba about Poland *as a country of one thousand and one nights*.

The Arabic tales are told for thirty months in Teatr 13 Rzędów which becomes his home, a tiny venue wherein, *through a small door, Barba enters a short narrow corridor, which also serves as a foyer and leads into a room which is no more than eighty square metres in size* (Barba 1999a: 20). The string of events, friendships, meetings, meaningful episodes, exchanges of ideas, books, and jokes catches the colours of the rainbow shining in the sky.

Dziady is the first performance by Grotowski that Barba sees and leaves him *indifferent*. His passionate love for Poland gradually fades away: *In this society which defined itself as socialist, his left-wing ideas collide with endless examples of injustice, abuse of power, bureaucracy, indifference and cynicism. His ingenuousness vanishes, and in its place he feels acquiescence and apathy creeping in* (Barba 1999a: 22). It is providence that, on an October day, makes Barba interrupt his journey to Cracow, get off the train in Opole and find his way to Teatr 13 Rzędów. And it is also providence which arranges the two young men to meet again at a bar in Cracow, where after hours of discussions, late at night, Grotowski proposes to work with him, as his assistant. At the end of January 1962, Barba begins his artistic adventure at Teatr 13 Rzędów. *From the first moment of his arrival, Grotowski hands him a 24-page pamphlet entitled Możliwość teatru, one half of it consisting of texts written by him and Ludwik Flaszen, which reveal main points of their vision of theatre* (Barba 1999a: 27). *His role as 'assistant director' in* Akropolis *and* Doctor Faustus *consists in sitting and watching the progress of rehearsals and training sessions, making comments, expressing doubts, asking for explanations, making suggestions* (Barba 1999a: 34). July-December 1963 is the time for his journey to India where he studies Kathakali for three weeks, *noting down the physical exercises, those for developing the mobility of the eyes and of the facial muscles, and the gaits* (Barba 1999a: 53); some of the exercises are used in training for a short period of time.

So, as in a fairy tale, the dawn breaks, clearing the initiation path of the two rebels menaced by faceless future dangers. The seeds of rebellion germinate in a socialist Poland *during a period in its history which is marked by the dreariness of a police regime and by the fervour of an intellectual and artistic life that is at the same time a liberating cry and a tireless fashioning of liberty* (Barba 1999a: 10). They spend nights on end in the station restaurant in Opole, in Grotowski's small room crammed with books or in Barba's spacious room that is, in their *house of dreams* (Barba 2010b: 27), where they focus, among jokes and ironic comments, on the themes and books they are interested in: Hinduism, Ramakrishna, Ramana Maharshi, Ernest Renan, *Life of Jesus*, the techniques of Gurdjieff and Ouspensky, alchemy, shamanism, trance, rituals, the *misterium tremendum et fascinans*, Jung, Durkheim, Lévy-Bruhl, Mauss, Levi-Strauss, Caillois, Bachelard and Eliade. In this regard, Barba tells us: "Their texts made us reflect out loud, and we used ourselves and our own experiences to investigate the fertile zone of 'archetypes', of 'collective representations', of 'wild thought'. We commented on them, paraphrased them; they inspired in us endless suppositions and hypotheses. These were the sources we tapped in an unceasing reformulation of a vision of theatre" (Barba 1999a: 50). Besides, the two young men, endowed with exceptional creative and intellectual capacities, analyse and confront their work with that of Stanislavsky, Meyerhold, Vachtangov, Dullin, Delsarte, Marcel Marceau, also showing deep interest in the Asian theatre. To revolutionise the theatre involves more than to acquire a set of professional *know-hows* necessary to create the scenic space, costume, light, music, mask, to deal with a certain text, or to use certain acting techniques. Passion, rigorous study and incessant research play an important part in the foundation of a vision of theatre.

Grotowski pursues "the vision of an actor capable of creating 'signs', true visible, auditory and above all psychic shocks for the spectator and for the collective imagination. The search for these 'signs' whose dynamism is imbued with associations is not based on psychology or the mechanics of cause and effect, but on a theatrical logic. This logic is rooted in organic coherence and presupposes a physical and psychic discipline, in other words a technique. The mastery over this technique becomes a personal process which makes actors discover their own interior flora and fauna, introducing them to the shared territory of the collective imagination" (Barba 1999a: 40). At the same time, Barba strives assiduously "to find terms that are both appropriate and suggestive to epitomise the features of this new theatre" (Barba 1999a: 50) and he succeeds admirably inventing in his writings expressions such as "theatre as an anthropological expedition, performance as psychomachia, as a clash between, on the one hand, the psychic process of the actors as they lay themselves bare and, on the other, the spectators who want to defend their certainties and psychic wellbeing"; he also uses "the expression 'self-penetration' to characterise the actor's inner process in this theatre which was not yet defined as 'poor'" (Barba 1999a: 50).

The fact that Jerzy Grotowski's performances, often censored and ignored, succeeded not only to stir a tremendous national interest but also to enjoy recognition worldwide, is a miracle. But this miracle would not have been accomplished without Eugenio Barba's fundamental contribution. Taking direct contact with the perfidious forms of the Polish censorship, he fights fiercely against the censors' attempts to bury alive Grotowski's new, revolutionising way of thinking and making theatre. Grotowski's productions, not being recognised by the representatives of the mainstream, are constantly threatened to be thrown forever in the common grave of the theatre. At the direction of the theatre, besides Grotowski, is Ludwik Flaszen "considered to be one of the best literary and theatre critics", whose "first book *The Head and The Wall* had been confiscated by the censors. However, a few rare copies circulated underground, revealing Flaszen's critical attitude towards official literature and its criteria" (Barba 1999a: 19). But their *underground resistance* proves powerless. The act of informing theatre personalities about their work becomes an essential point in Barba's strategies. In this respect, Raymonde and Valentin Temkine play a significant part in supporting Grotowski's work. But it is Barba who stays by his side in a Poland which "was a prison, where you could neither have a passport nor travel abroad as could citizens in capitalist Europe" (Barba 1999a: 25), decisively contributing to the consolidation of his artistic destiny as a world-famous personality. To make Grotowski's research and performances known, Barba publishes numerous articles on Grotowski's theories and productions, the booklets *Expériences du théâtre laboratoire 13 Rzędów* and *Le théâtre comme auto-pénétration collective* (Barba 1999a: 59); he collaborates with *Sipario* magazine which dedicates an issue to the Polish theatre; in 1965, he publishes *Alla ricerca del teatro perduto* (*In Search of a Lost Theatre*), a book about Grotowski and the group work in Opole; he looks for allies for support in Poland and abroad; he contributes majorly to the organisation of the Teatr 13 Rzędów's tour with *Doctor Faustus* during the Tenth Congress of the ITI, the International Theatre Institute, held in Warsaw, 1963, which stands out as an important moment in Grotowski's and his actors' future worldwide recognition. In February 1966, he organises the first tour of Teatr-Laboratorium abroad; between

1966-1969 he organises seminars in Holstebro in which Grotowski participates together with other artists; he publishes texts written by or about Grotowski in several issues of the magazine *Teatrets Teori og Teknikk* and in 1968 the first English version of Grotowski's book *Towards a Poor Theatre* initially conceived as issue number 7 of the TTT (*Teatrets Teori og Teknikk*), *an anthology in English of texts by various authors* (Barba 1999a: 99). In this respect, Barba asserts: "None of my acquaintances escaped my agitprop zeal and missionary activism for the Theatre's New Testament" (Barba 1999a: 60). I repeat, his contribution to the national and international recognition of Grotowski's and his actors' work is priceless. Why does Barba all this for Grotowski? Barba himself tells us: "I firmly believed that Grotowski's way of thinking would shake the ancient edifice of theories and routines, that his words were the Word, the New Testament of the Theatre. I wanted to witness, to spread the Word, to act as a proselyte" (Barba 1999a: 50-51).

The remarkable friendship between the two masters is an undeniable example of a spiritual bond that transcends spatial and temporal limits. Sharing a *common language* (Barba 1999a: 9), the language of the artist, they *weave the web of their relationship* "spinning it over an abyss of dark and luminous forces – longings, needs and certainties. An inner space to which we can give different names: a journey into the depths of our own being, or an escape from it" (Barba 1999a: 23). It is the language which speaks about revolt and submission, freedom and constraint, construction and destruction, sameness and difference. This living bond involves common experiences, mutual stimulations required in times of doubt or fear, renunciation or resignation. Even though Barba and Grotowski share questions on theatre, they give different answers, as each of them follows his path of creative thinking.

Land of Ashes and Diamonds speaks about the profound symbiotic relationship established between two persons: *Grotowski, through theatre technique, always conducted his very personal research in a profound symbiotic relationship with another person. When Barba left Opole, after a period of nearly three years, he embarked on this sort of relationship with Ryszard Cieślak. The result was extraordinary:* The Constant Prince. [...] *From 1962 to 1964 Barba was this privileged companion* (Barba 1999a: 26). At the same time, the book speaks about their resistance to the disfiguring razor of censorship and their keenness to freely give expression to the theatre as they see it. 1964-1966: *For Grotowski these were the years preceding the explosion of his fame, and for Barba those of the foundation and establishment of Odin Teatret in Oslo, Norway, and then in Holstebro, Denmark* (Barba 1999a: 9).

On October 1st 1964, Eugenio Barba creates Odin Teatret, in Oslo, together with young people who were rejected by the national theatre school. In June 1966, Odin Teatret moves to Holstebro in Denmark as the municipality offers them an empty farm, on the outskirts of the town, which today is a castle of the world theatre, where the director *does not resolve problems, but creates problems for himself, for the actors and for the spectators* (Barba 1999a: 104).

Eugenio Barba's actions speak for themselves gathering around the idea of the openness of one human being to another human being, emphasising the necessity to recognise the value of the other's work, whether he is your master, *the guru with many faces* (Barba 2000b: 18) or not, and to treat him with love, respect and generosity.

But, as the story goes on, one day, the master, if we enjoy the privilege to have a master, disappears. His image, slowly, fades away, and only the scent of his skin or the twinkle in his eyes is kept in a remote chamber of our memories. From his living presence, all that is left is a term, a model, a point of reference, or an abstract notion. And we start asking ourselves: "Who is this distant and invisible master? The professional superego? The person, or collection of people who have consciously or unconsciously led us to incorporate certain tensions that become the rudder for our most secret impulses, our most extreme decisions, our most punctilious achievements? Why does the master vanish? To let us know that from now on we are able to live without him, that we have become him or that what is essential is concealed *behind* his image" (Barba 1999a: 106)?

The director-playwright

"PLAYGOER: And you consider that the stage-director is a craftsman and not an artist?

STAGE-DIRECTOR: When he interprets the plays of the dramatist by means of his actors, his scene-painters, and his other craftsmen, then he is a craftsman – a master craftsman; when he will have mastered the uses of actions, words, line, colour, and rhythm, then he may become an artist. Then we shall no longer need the assistance of the playwright – for our art will then be self-reliant.

PLAYGOER: Is your belief in a Renaissance of the art based on your belief in the Renaissance of the stage director?

STAGE-DIRECTOR: Yes, certainly, most certainly." (Craig 1957: 148)

Although Eugenio Barba does not aim *to pass on a style, create a school or a method, or define a personal aesthetic* (Barba 2010a: XV), he succeeds both in defining universal principles of directing and dramaturgy and creating theatrical values shared by theatre people all over the world. His way of thinking and making theatre reveals the nature of the theatre artist who freely, that is unconstrained by fashion trends and successful theatrical recipes, devises new modes of understanding and practising the theatre craft. Revisiting the notion of performance, he approaches it from the perspective of the coexistence of opposites: the *obscure forces* and the *orderly thinking*, the *vision* and the *technique*, the *interior freedom* and the *chaining to the oar of the craft*.

For Barba, the dramaturgy, a *science of the stage* created entirely by the *artists of the stage*, consists in the *work of the actions*: "In a performance, actions (that is, all that has to do with the dramaturgy) are not only what is said and done, but also the sounds, the lights and the changes in space. At a higher level of organisation, actions are the episodes of the story or the different facets of a situation, the arches of time between two accents of the performance, between two changes in the space – or even the evolution of the musical score, the light changes, and the variations of rhythm and intensity which a performer develops following certain precise physical themes (ways of walking, of handling props, of using make-up or costume). The objects used in the performance are also *actions*. They are transformed, they acquire different meanings and different emotive colourations. All the relationships, all the interactions between the characters or between the characters and the lights, the sounds and the space, are actions. Everything that works directly on the spectators' attention, on their understanding, their emotions, their kinaesthesia is an action. [...] What is important is to observe that the actions come into play only when they are woven together, when they become texture: 'text'" (Barba-Savarese 2006: 66). Franco Ruffini, in his exceptional study *The Culture of the Text and the Culture of the Stage* (Barba-Savarese 2006: 270-274), refers amply to Eugenio Barba's *new theatre*.

Before giving names to his discoveries, the director-playwright fills with *his own sense* the terms that for him are related to the *essence of the theatre*: revolt, empty ritual, dissidence, vulnerability, transcendence-superstition, diversity, refusal, craft, floating island, barter, emigration, wound, origin, serendipity; he is also fascinated by the *terms that refer to the aspects of the craft*: sats, kraft, organic effect, energy, rhythm, flow, dramaturgy, dance (Barba 2010a: 2-3). As he remarks, he seldom used the term *dramaturgy* at the beginning of his practical work *when his efforts were concentrated on how he could provoke personal reactions in the actors and orchestrate these in a performance, which did not imitate life, but possessed a life of its own* (Barba 2010a: 8). At the end of the 1970s, Barba intensifies his research on *identifying and comparing certain technical principles belonging to actors and dancers from various genres, a field of study which he calls theatre anthropology,* and defines dramaturgy. In this regard, the director asserts: "Trying to explain in my own words the technical terminology of my own theatre tradition, I defined 'dramaturgy' according to its etymology: *drama-ergon*, the work of the actions. Or rather: the way the actor's actions enter into work. For me, dramaturgy was not a procedure belonging only to literature, but a technical operation which was inherent in the weaving and growth of a performance and its different components" (Barba 2010a: 8). Interested in the *effectiveness of a way of seeing which takes into account different and overlapping logics*, he comes to analyse the 'layered nature of the performance' identifying *on the one hand, the dramaturgy of the performance as plot, as a weaving of different threads in a concatenation and simultaneity of different actions or episodes, and on the other, the simultaneous presence in depth of different layers, each endowed with its own logic and peculiar way of manifesting its life* (Barba 2010a: 9-10). The three levels of organisation of the dramaturgy which mostly stir his interest are the level of the *organic* or *dynamic dramaturgy*, the level of the *narrative dramaturgy* and the level of the *evocative dramaturgy*. *He isolates the levels artificially and thinks about them separately* (Barba 2010a: 10) as if each level has its own life independent of the others; as if each level is a funnel which produces energies and meanings. During the process of working on the dramaturgy of the performance, the director-playwright operates transplantations of meanings, makes changes in the order of the actions and scenes, transfers actions from a scene to another, creates *knots and reversals*. The objective of his montage consists in the *distillation of the 'complex' relationships capable of 'overturning' the obvious relationships*. At the level of the *organic dramaturgy*, he works with *physical and vocal actions, costumes, objects, music, sounds, lights, spatial features*; at the level of the *narrative dramaturgy*, with *characters, stories, texts, events, iconographic references*; at the level of the *evocative dramaturgy*, he concentrates on *the work necessary to make the same performance reverberate differently in the spectators' biographical caverns* (Barba 2010a: 10).

After his first three performances, Barba definitively renounces the pre-existing written text and works on his dramaturgy based on themes which preoccupy him. These themes, such as initiation, progress, war, sacrifice, death, which in the early stage of his research on dramaturgy revolve around "the relationship between society and the individual, injustice, meaningless violence, cruelty and struggle" (Nagel Rasmussen 2018: 57), are *really big topics* "over which oceans of blood and ink have been spilled, but they are really big topics for one reason alone: each is a powerful source of human emotion. If they didn't make us *feel* uplifted, desperate, thankful, and hopeless, we would keep all that ink and blood to ourselves" (Gilbert 2006). As Barba *feels the need to deal with his narrative materials as if they were fragments of a myth or limbs of an archetype* (Barba 2010a: 106), during his working process, he creates *dynamic images* (Jung), archetypes, such as *the shadow, the animal, the wise old man, the anima, the mother, the child* (Jung). In his performances, we notice the presence of the shadow, that is *the most dangerous aspect of the dark half of man* (Jung), in *Andersen's Dream*; of the Shaman, "the primitive tribal magician or medicine man, a peculiarly gifted individual invested with magical power" (Jung 1928: 102), in *Come! And the Day Will Be Ours* and of the Black Madonna, *a figure who appears as dark-skinned* (Jung 1928: 102), in *The Chronic Life*; of the animal in *Don Giovanni all'Inferno;* of the mother in *Kaosmos* and in *The Chronic Life*. At the same time, Barba builds *archetypal presences* such as the *Man-from-the-country* and the *Man-who-does-not-want-to-die*. Mythical destinies and a vision of a future world marked by a devastating sadness are present in *The Chronic Life*. Here we have the mother / the Widow of a Basque Officer who puts a gun in the hands of a child / the Young Colombian to pull the trigger and commit a crime; the Black Madonna, looking like a senile old woman with her black face and red tongue, sometimes limping and sometimes enjoying rocking on a wooden horse, seems to be deprived of her magical powers; the Rock Musician no longer resembles a prophet-bard, no longer tells stories about gods and heroes, but blaming himself and others for everything that has gone wrong in his life, tells us the story of his failures; the Danish Lawyer, who reminds us of the ferryman who takes one to the World of the Dead, here stamps the visa into one's passport to enter the Wonderland; the Rumanian Housewife who bears a striking resemblance to the angel who falls from heaven because she feels too tired to continue to fly. *The Chronic Life* can be seen as a performance in which "the myth reveals itself as a problematic example, an enigmatic dimension of existence" (Barba 2002a: 19).

Regarding Barba's dramaturgy, we no longer deal with *a dissection of a corpse, the pre-existing text, but with a vivisection of a living material, the actor.* We no longer deal with working on a dramatic or literary text, but with working with narrative sources. We no longer deal with contemporizing ancient myths, but with creating myths of our time. At the same time, in his dramaturgy, the director-playwright reveals the characteristics of human nature and human condition, the contemporary individual's nostalgia for Paradise, his hunger for rediscovering the patch of honour buried in his daily shopping bag. A possible reason why Barba creates *simultaneous scenes* is that he realises that a performance based on a linear narrative which follows the direct causality pattern is marked by *predictability*. A subtle observer of the changes occurred in today's society, the director analyses the complexity of the human relationships and the transformations of the actual individual, aiming to tell a *story behind every action,* to create scenes which carry both the patina of the past and the fragrance of the future, *to make the invisible visible*, to devise a performance open to the spectators' countless interpretations. For Barba, *the work on the narrative level does not aim to set up a plot which the spectator will understand during the performance: only one story for all the spectators. He has a tendency to create conditions in which every single spectator can read his own personal story into the performance* (Barba 2010a: 88). When he starts working on a performance, *the director-playwright knows neither its story nor its purpose*: "At Odin Teatret, for example, there is no preliminary work on the text or on 'the character', understood as a part of a dramatic organism with pre-defined and well delineated contours. It is the performance itself, when the rehearsals are over, which defines the characters and their relationships. There is no play, text or subject however brief. The starting point is not a scenario explaining to the actors the existing relationships and situations, scene by scene, between the different *dramatis personae*. There is nothing to help the actors to foresee how the plot will develop and end. Nobody knows in advance the story or its purpose" (Taviani 2011: 20-21). During the working process, *the Disorder and the Error, children of Silence, two angels with the appearance of hooligans* (Barba 2010a: 17) are meant to guide the director on his way to the *Principalities of shadows and Powers and Possibilities* (Craig 1957: 265) helping him to discover the hidden story of the performance.

Through *the organic dramaturgy-the performance's nervous system which makes the spectators dance kinaesthetically on their seat, through the narrative dramaturgy-the cortex which releases conjectures, thoughts, doubts, evaluations, questions, and through the evocative dramaturgy-that part of us which lives in exile within us and makes us live a 'change of state'* (Barba 2010a: 10-11), Barba addresses the spectator as a *whole*, concomitantly to his mind and senses, intellect and affect. During the privileged space and time of rehearsals, the director *imagines scenes and compositions and – still in his imagination – destroys them. Imagining and destroying are complementary actions for a director like him, to whom experience has taught that one way to succeed is voluntarily to take the wrong road, and that the correct solution is the unexpected one, welling up with the convincing power of serendipity* (Taviani 2011: 17).

Order and Disorder are not two opposing options, but two poles which coexist and stimulate each other. The quality of the tension created between them provides the level of fertility of the creative process (Barba 2012a: 114).

Both the Disorder, *that logic and that rigour which provoke the 'experience of bewilderment' in the director and in the spectator, that 'irruption of an energy that confronts us with the unknown'* (Barba 2010a: 17), and the order are essential in Barba's working process. Extrapolating, it is as if during this process the *old scenic world* disintegrates into particles which gradually compose a *new scenic world*. Leaving behind the *known* and stepping into the *unknown*, the director follows unexplored *creative paths*.

There are multitudes of possible interpretations of Barba's performances which sink their roots in related narrative sources. His performances make the spectator feel the impulse to become an *active* part and, as Artaud dreamed, the spectator becomes *active*. Antonin Artaud visualises *the concrete physical language of the stage, intended for the senses and independent of speech, which has first to satisfy the senses; there is a poetry of the senses as there is a poetry of language and this language created for the senses must from the outset be concerned with satisfying them; nevertheless this does not prevent it from developing later its full intellectual effect on all possible levels and in every direction* (Artaud 1958: 37-38). Barba creates *the concrete physical language of the stage* which speaks not only to *imagination and wit*, but also "to stupidity, to childish amazement, to a simple sensuality that appeals to our instincts, and to our impulse to raise one wing towards the sky, while the feathers of the other scratch ignoble graffiti on the dusty earth" (Barba 2006: 4).

So, we no longer deal with what we traditionally call dramaturgy, that is, with a theatre play written down on a sheet of paper by the playwright who dreams of the day when a director might become interested in putting it on stage.

We no longer deal with the adaptation of a text – poem, novel, short story, diary, biography – for a performance.

We no longer deal with the conventional situation in which the actor builds his character taking into consideration both the playwright's *didascalia* and the director's instructions.

We no longer deal with *the dialectics – the 'emaciated' text and the actor who incarnates the spirit of the text.*

Barba and his actors sometimes know neither the text nor the story of the performance they start to hunt.

The actor's dramaturgy is supposed to mean, firstly, the capacity to build the equivalent of the complexity which characterizes the action in life. This construction, which is perceived as a character, has to have a sensorial and mental impact on the spectator. The objective of the actor's dramaturgy is the capacity to stimulate affective reactions (Barba 1996a: 17). Master of the *technical discipline*, the Odin actor, creator of the organic dramaturgy, no longer approaches a character who has an independent existence in a dramatic text, no longer attempts to build it scenically, but creates the character according to his reactions to a certain theme proposed by Barba.

Nando Taviani, in *The Black Indies of Odin Teatret*, unveils a few characteristics of Eugenio Barba's process of creation: "In the periods when the process was hibernating, each actor worked out materials to propose to the director (costumes, masks, props, songs and music, texts to recite or to sing, silhouettes of characters, etc.). [...] They knew that the work on the new performance, accomplished in solitude, was a wasted effort. Perhaps a tenth of it or maybe nothing at all would be usable. But they also knew that *unusable* doesn't necessarily mean *useless*. However they were not able to orient themselves. Beyond the circle of their individual work they could see only darkness. Neither the actors nor their director-playwright had in their hands a 'production plan' delineating the plot, the texts and the scenes of the performance to come. Working in this way has become normal in the Odin enclave in the last twenty years. It is a way of proceeding in which every actor is responsible for his or her own personal path, refining it with extreme care like a detail whose only importance is that it be alive, before knowing the landscape of which it will be a part. The extreme precision of the details is connected with a similar extremist suspension of judgment regarding the context in which these details will acquire a sense of their own. [...] Every detail is a physical action precisely designed. It is not an empty, rootless sign that on its own is deprived of sense. It is the fruit of an imagination-in-action, rooted in the actor's physical-mental organism. More than a sign, it is a cell with a life of its own, although still not part of an organ and a destiny indicating its identity and belonging. An action-cell can be transplanted in different unprogrammed contexts. The director-playwright is responsible for this operation and acts, above all, as a transformer of meaning" (Taviani 2011: 17-20). By the term *the 'actor's dramaturgy'*, *Barba refers to the actor's creative contribution to the growth of a performance as well as to his ability to root what he recounts into a structure of organic actions* (Barba 2010a: 23). The organic actions, *by 'organic' Barba means the actions that unleash a kinaesthetic commitment and are sensorially convincing for the spectator, whatever the convention and genre used by the actor,* are the foundation of the performance and *have a great impact on the nervous system of the spectator* (Barba 2010a: 23). *The work of the actor appears to the director, who considers the performance as a 'living organism which communicates' and within which different dramaturgies cohabit, as a task which is no longer to justify a character's psychology, but to develop his own dramaturgy through physical and vocal actions* (Barba 2010a: 24).

In 1907, in *The Actor and the Über-marionette*, Edward Gordon Craig visualises the future of the actor-artist calling him the Über-marionette. After his concept caused waves of indignation among the colleagues in the guild who cried out: "And what, pray, is this monster the Über-marionette?", Craig put it plainly: "The Über-marionette is the actor plus fire, minus egoism: the fire of the gods and demons, without the smoke and steam of mortality. The literal ones took me to mean pieces of wood one foot in height; that infuriated them; they talked of it for ten years as a mad, a wrong, an insulting idea" (Craig 1957: IX-X). Raising questions about the condition of the actor as artist, Craig foresees a possibility through which the actors surpassing the boundaries of their craft enter art: "They must create for themselves a new form of acting, consisting for the main part of symbolical gesture. Today they *impersonate* and interpret; tomorrow they must *represent* and interpret; and the third day they must create" (Craig 1957: 61). To create, the actor must expand and enrich his inner world and constantly train his mind and body of *physical athlete*. To create his character sometimes means not only to make use of episodes from his own biography but also to construct a fictional world in which he and his character live in symbiosis. During his quest, it is as if the actor searches for his character through the galleries of his chaotic, raw creative material of which he makes a sculpture, breathing life into it. Eleonora Duse speaks about the actors who have to die of plague for the theatre to be regenerated, Craig speaks about the actors who should disappear and be replaced with Über-marionette. The Odin actor incarnates Craig's dream: the actor-artist, a living scenic presence, concomitantly engaging his mind and body *to create symbolic actions*, "For not only is Symbolism at the roots of all art, it is at the roots of all life, it is only by means of symbols that life becomes possible for us; we employ them all the time" (Craig 1957: 293-294).

And so we know that the actor acts in the space-time of the performance speaking the language of the symbol, that is the language which the other/spectator knows it and recognises it as such. A universal language spoken in the kingdom of the profound existential states. A language in which what we call the spoken word is, for Joe Chaikin, *the creation of a universe of the word*, as he observes that *if we can utter the word splendour not only to express its idea, but also to give rise to splendour, then the voice creates beyond word* (Chaikin 1973: 54).

During the individual improvisations, the actor elaborates *his score, an objective demonstration of his subjective world* (Barba 2010a: 28), which is rooted in his *underscore, a technical element belonging to his particular creative logic* (Barba 2010a: 29), which *may consist in a rhythm, a song, a particular way of breathing, an action that is assimilated and miniaturised by the actor, an action which he does not display but whose dynamism guides him even in quasi-immobility* (Barba 2012a: 85). Then, during rehearsals, the director-playwright works on the actor's score "even changing it radically, until it becomes a coherent sequence of dynamic peripeteias: *bios* (life), scenic presence ready to represent and acquire a meaning by being connected to a text, to the score of another actor, to an object, a melody or a light" (Barba 2010a: 30-31). The scores are conceived both with a life of their own as well as in close relationships and reciprocal influences.

"The performance dances not only on the level of energy but also on the narrative level. It is its *meaning* which dances, sometimes explicitly, sometimes covertly and secretly, open to the free associations of some spectators, while ambiguous and unrecognisable for others." (Barba 1999b: 245)

Significant for Barba's dramaturgical process is the text he writes in 1985 about *The Gospel according to Oxyrhincus*: "When I started work on the production whose final title was *Oxyrhincus Evangeliet*, there was neither a written text nor a scenario – not even a single guiding theme. [...] There was an interweaving of themes, of historical and mythical figures taken from different periods and distant cultures, of contemporary political personalities and characters from novels. All these began to people my mental space and, through the actors, the material space of the theatre. In this double space, the paths of the various protagonists began to intertwine: an unforeseen story was born. My suggestions and the improvisations of the actors, our reciprocal intuition together with fortuitous discoveries, slowly crystallised into patterns of actions, relationships and situations which were often based on simultaneity. The vocal universe of the production was composed at this stage in the work. I wrote some texts which evoked the logic and the images of popular ballads about Brazilian outlaws or the Kabbalah, contemporary political speeches or love poems, anecdotes about Hassidic Rabbis or mediaeval chronicles, sometimes reinvented through the improvisations of the actors. All these texts were 'translated': throughout the performance the actors speak the language of Oxyrhincus, the Hellenistic city on the Nile where three fragments of apocryphal gospels were discovered. I then took the texts spoken by the actors, retranslated them into my own language – Italian – and composed a play which attempts to transfer to the linear dimension of the written language the flow of a story proceeding not by transitions but by jumps" (Barba 1985a).

Since the beginning of his extraordinary journey through the *Country of Theatre*, with the performance *Ornitofilene*, 1965, Barba *works with the text* as he re-elaborates completely Jens Bjørneboe's text being *interested in the subliminal dimension, and not in the illustration or comment on the written word* (Nagel Rasmussen 2018: 38). This re-elaboration requires the invention of scenes which do not exist in the original text; the scenes are called by the director "warm scenes" (Nagel Rasmussen 2018: 38) and are built through improvisations. Also from the start, it is noticeable that *there are themes that come up again and again in his productions*. Such a theme is that of self-flagellation present in *Ornitofilene* and reiterated in the Rock Musician's (self)flagellation scene in *The Chronic Life*. For Barba, to extract *archetypal situations* from his own biography and life experience as well as from the biographies and works of cultural and historical figures is also a constant way of thinking up his dramaturgy.

Kaspariana, 1967, is based on a long poem written by Ole Sarvig. There are major differences between Jens Bjørneboe's dramatic piece for *Ornitofilene* and the text around which the second performance is built, as the director remarks: "There wasn't the slightest indication as to which was the first, second or third scene. There was no definition or profile of the play's characters. Atmosphere was created through words. It was very poetic but devoid of dramatic impact. We were faced with a whole series of 'holes' in the story which we ourselves had to fill in" (Nagel Rasmussen 2018: 53-54). Creating scenes which gravitate towards the human being's stages of life, Barba introduces another theme that crosses his dramaturgy, the *life of the Son of Man*, of the individual who is sacrificed by the society. The *figure who is Kaspar Hauser but also Christ* (Nagel Rasmussen 2018: 54) corresponds to the Man-who-does-not-want-to-die, in *Kaosmos*, and to the Young Colombian who does not integrate into a society ironically called Wonderland, in *The Chronic Life*. Archetypal situations, *stereotypes which always contain an archetypal element* (Nagel Rasmussen 2018: 56), archetypes which "manifest themselves subjectively in such things as dreams, fantasies, writing, poetry, painting and objectively in such collective representations as myths, rituals, and cultural symbols" (Turner 1988: 173) are present in Barba's dramaturgy which at the narrative level is often based on poetic words and micro-sequences purposely built as oniric images meant to open the door to the individual and collective unconscious. In this regard, the myth of Christ, the Greek myths, the Ritual of the Disorder, the Ritual of the Door are subject to minutious investigations. In his dramaturgy, the director raises questions about the life of the myth, about the connections between the ancient Greek myths and the modern/contemporary myths, stories which embrace each other over millennia, poured in scenic forms intended to reflect the myths of our days. The director-playwright's narrative sources are rooted in distant histories, for example, the life of Christ, in recent histories, such as, the Warsaw Uprising, as well as in his personal experiences as *it has always been important to him to be able to blend personal experience with history – History with a capital H* (Nagel Rasmussen 2018: 70).

In *My Father's House*, 1972, the director gives free rein to his imagination; as a result "It is impossible to put a finger on anything in particular and say, *that* is Dostoevsky, or here we have characters from his novels or episodes from his life. Nevertheless, he is present in every thread of this intricately woven performance" (Nagel Rasmussen 2018: 100). In this performance *the actors' individual improvisations are pieced together/edited by the director, forming a dynamic pattern of actions* (Nagel Rasmussen 2018: 99). The first improvisation, '*Dostoevsky's father's house', is followed by many others inspired by historical and literary facts from the period of the Russian author, as well as by episodes from the actors' and Barba's contemporary history* (Barba 2010a: 114).

Carpignano, May 1974, is the place for new revelations. The location, initially chosen for training and rehearsals for the new performance *Come! And the Day Will Be Ours*, 1976, turns out to be an ideal space for meditation, research and barter. Here the idea and practice of *barter*, an essential element in the theatre anthropology, take roots, and also here the director and his actors create the performance *The Book of Dances* based on training exercises. Even though it *does not tell a story, because of its rhythm, power and presence, the performance is striking and makes an impression on people who have never experienced theatre before* (Nagel Rasmussen 2018: 110). The organic connections between the training exercises and the scenic actions enrich and nuance the scenic language.

Beginning with *Come! And the Day Will Be Ours,* the director-playwright's preoccupations focus on *the level in a performance that involves the senses* identifying and exploiting particular ways to awaken the spectator's senses: "certain colours in the costumes, the sound of the music, the emotional effect of the songs. The dynamic quality of the actions, the 'dancing energy' of the actors, the controlled and unrestrained outbursts, voices used like colours and brush-strokes in Van Gogh's paintings. The whole magnificent, living dance of sats and impulses. The texts too, however brief, should preferably have the same immediacy and depth as a Zen poem: 'Dark is a way – and light is a place', for example" (Nagel Rasmussen 2018: 122). The *same immediacy and depth* are to be found also in the actors' lines in *The Chronic Life,* for example: *To believe in love is the key.* In this world of impulses, rhythms and unleashed energies, the director's *strength* is, as Iben Nagel Rasmussen notes in *The Blind Horse,* "the ability to distil living materials and to subordinate them to the theme's strict objective without, however, jeopardising their vitality" (Nagel Rasmussen 2018: 133); the theme in *Come! And the Day Will Be Ours* revolves around *the incertitude and the intransigence of the European immigrants, poor or persecuted, entwined with the incertitude and the intransigence of the native populations of the American continent* (Barba 2010b: 20).

Eugenio Barba face-to-face with Bertolt Brecht: in *Brecht's Ashes,* the first version in 1980, the second version in 1982, the director-playwright articulates the scenic language at the confluence of the impressions made upon him by Brecht's work. In this case, *theatre, for Barba, is synonymous with revolt which he finds in the theatre of Brecht, in his exhortation to commitment and struggle against injustice and indifference* (Barba 2010a: 16). In Brecht's writings, as Ian Watson remarks, Barba recognises the social and political role of the theatre whose objective is to awaken the spectator's consciousness. Barba devises the performance in order to reflect the Brechtian idea of non-involvement in illusion, conferring it the quality to provoke both in the actor and in the spectator the need to distance themselves from the everyday reality to reach a trans-historical reality: "Toward the end of *Brecht's Ashes 2* there was a scene in which a cook abandoned her cooking and walked around the stage singing. As a backdrop to her song, Brecht and a musician worked together on another song at an organ in a corner of the stage, while the rest of the cast sat in silence around a sofa in a tableau reminiscent of Berlin's decadent 1930s observing everything. The lights brightened and the *Threepenny Opera's* Mackie Messer (one of the leading characters in *Brecht's Ashes 2*) stepped out of the tableau and announced that Brecht had returned to a recently liberated East Germany. He then danced with another of Brecht's characters who played an important role in Barba's production, Kattrin from *Mother Courage*, while displaying a copy of *Pravda* as the others cleaned the stage. The dancing became more frenzied as the cleaning neared completion, until suddenly Messer stuffed the copy of *Pravda* into Kattrin's mouth and the lights went out" (Watson 1993: 93-94). One of the challenges the director faces is *how to visualise and produce Brecht's alienation effect*. If the technique of *inversion* in *The Chronic Life* sometimes generates an alienation effect, in *Brecht's Ashes* this effect is achieved first of all by reiterating the same text in different languages and using different registers: "Mack-the-Knife would translate everything that Brecht said into Danish, English or Italian, according to the country in which we were performing. In this way Mack-the-Knife would always be able to relate to what Brecht said with a form of ironic distance. He could play down or ridicule a sentence, or present one of Brecht's statements in such a way as to make it appear in a different light. That was one possible alienation effect. Everything that might have seemed pathetic or bombastic about Brecht's character was broken down" (Nagel Rasmussen 2018: 154).

Barba's work on dramaturgy reaches a point when the director asks himself new questions such as: "Would it be possible, dramaturgically speaking, to create a performance consisting of different threads, different events and stories that are woven together? Could I create a piece in which the actions were concrete and precise, yet at the same time so ambiguous as to be interpreted as different stories according to the titles I gave them?" (Nagel Rasmussen 2018: 165) At this stage, he makes use of the actors' capacity to distance themselves from their intense emotions, bringing into play mostly their intellective ability. As a consequence, for *The Gospel according to Oxyrhincus*, Barba is preoccupied with a *question of technical nature*: "were the actors capable of creating physical scores that were 'cold' to start with, and then giving them a 'soul' only in a later phase? We used the term *marble*. The actors' sequences of set actions were marble to be worked on during rehearsals, just as a sculptor works on his block of marble" (Nagel Rasmussen 2018: 166). With *The Gospel according to Oxyrhincus*, the director makes changes in his working process; *after the actors have repeated their sequences individually, he begins his elaboration so that their sequences could be placed in relationship to the text or to the numerous performing situations* (Nagel Rasmussen 2018: 166).

When referring to the narrative dramaturgy, in his book *On Directing and Dramaturgy: Burning the House,* Barba remarks: "After *My Father's House,* I was aware that a performance does not recount only *one* subject which I had interpreted, denied or grafted onto personal or historical experiences. The spectators, too, didn't filter an identical story through the actions of the same performance. Slowly an axiom began to coagulate in my mind: the narrative dramaturgy must be thought in the plural – more subjects, more perspectives, more stories" (Barba 2010a: 116). Besides thinking the narrative dramaturgy *in the plural*, Barba reflects upon the nature and condition of the spectator noticing that the spectator is also *in the plural*: "We say 'spectator' and we think of a unitary personality. It is not so: the spectator is always plural. When I think about myself as a spectator, I recognise the simultaneous presence of many voices speaking in unison, some domineering, others for the most part silenced, buried under my cultural prejudices. The latter are the coarsest, but they too have their own wisdom" (Barba 2006: 4). A single narrative thread, even if intelligently concocted, preserves its grain of *predictability* leaving the spectator in a so-called inner *security* state. *The feeling of being unsettled, the experiencing of a change of state* occur only if the dramaturgical tools are used in order to *provoke* powerful reactions in the spectator taking him by surprise. The *actions-ideograms,* the *dramaturgical knots,* the *poetic words,* the *organic links* between the physical and vocal actions, the *simultaneities* contribute to the creation of the *narrative dramaturgy in the plural*. A dramaturgy which speaks to us through its myriads of meanings, extraordinariness, unusualness, unexpectedness, unpredictability, ambiguity.

In his dramaturgical quest, Barba is attracted by *the destinies of historical and fictitious characters who can speak to each other only in our imagination* (Barba 2010a: 142); by the fascinating figures of Alcestis, Admetus, Antigone, Joan of Arc, Cassandra, Oedipus, Orpheus, Medea, Daedalus, Odysseus; by the destinies and works of Stanislavsky, Craig, Artaud, Brecht; by the figures of dictators but also of heroes whose names and heroic acts are constantly menaced to be forgotten, swallowed by the flowing sands of the history. However, during the preparation for the production *Talabot*, the director *becomes fascinated with the idea of building the action around a living person* (Nagel Rasmussen 2018: 174); *now he asks himself how to use a simple story, that of the Danish anthropologist Kirsten Hastrup, and give it a mythical ring* (Nagel Rasmussen 2018: 174). So, he embarks together with his actors on *Talabot*, the ship that dreaming of Ramakrishna he took in his youth. On their artistic journey, one of the challenges the director is confronted with is *how to transform an everyday sequence of events into a mythical account* (Nagel Rasmussen 2018: 175).

Kaosmos, 1993, has its point of departure in improvisations on *the three births of a wolf; the actors are also asked to create knots which must have the property of a corpse which swells up on the margin of the road: it is dead but at the same time it is full of life; and to write 'words in freedom', which are the words that the poet liberates from their univocal meaning giving them the freedom to signify more, words that will become actions* (Carreri 2007: 146). The performance covertly tells us about the Son of Man: "Torgeir [Wethal] is a Christ figure who goes unnoticed. He performs miracles, quotes the Scriptures, yet no one understands that the Son of God is among them" (Nagel Rasmussen 2018: 197). Miracles. Miracles happen both in *Kaosmos* and in *The Chronic Life*. In *Kaosmos* the miracle is performed in "the final scene in which the corn – which had been strewn over the frame of the open door as it lay on the ground – rose up as the door was closed" (Nagel Rasmussen 2018: 198). In *The Chronic Life* the miracle is accomplished also in the final scene in which the Young Colombian comes back to life after a long, death-like sleep.

In *Mythos*, 1998, the director-playwright works on Henrik Nordbrandt's poems. For this production, Barba seems to be interested in investigating the theme of *immortality* as "Around the corpse of a revolutionary are gathered the characters of the Greek myths. They take possession of him and introduce him to their immortality" (Nagel Rasmussen 2018: 209). It is a theme which raises questions about the life of the myth and its hero and also about the contemporaries' ways of approaching the mysteries of the ancient stories: *Maybe myth is the burning bush that illuminates one face of our experience, the most intimate, the most secret, inexplicable even to ourselves. Do myths die? Are they buried or hidden? Are they reborn to intensify the existence of the new myths? What is a myth? A myth can be a story that encloses a kernel of timeless truth, a problematic example, a wound that never stops bleeding in a shadowy zone of each individual, each epoch. A myth can also be a narrative deprived of truth, or else it can be a dense distillation of truth. There is another possibility: it can be that a historical fact has become a myth* (Nagel Rasmussen 2018: 213). We know that there is no *youth without age and life without death* but in myths and fairy tales; however, it is impossible not to admit our need for stories that fascinate us with their ancient beauty and enigmas.

Strongly attracted both by the power of the emotions (identification) and the power of the mind (alienation), Barba continuously expands his vision and explores the fascinating realms of dream, myth, fairy tale, personal and collective unconscious. At the same time, he creates the necessary working space for the actor to succeed in penetrating his intimate nature. During his process of self-discovery, sometimes the actor enters into a state of *active meditation* which leads him to an awareness of thoughts and emotions. In this respect, Torgeir Wethal's reflections come to my mind. Here is what the actor tells us:

"In my first work diary, in the autumn of 1964, I wrote:

> 'With regard to *études*:
> 1. Feel before expressing something.
> 2. Observe and see in detail before describing what you have seen.
> 3. Listen before replying.
> 4. Sight – hearing – taste – smell – touch: these senses must be taken into consideration and be constantly active'.

[…] The words of 1964 are still valid. And they've been at the core of my way of improvising for years, even though their content gradually came from bigger and more complex worlds than at the beginning. I have thus often been confronted by the unknown and the unconscious. My reaction to these meetings caused me to perform actions in a way that previously I would not have been able to identify as being mine. […]

Eugenio [Barba] attempted to explain to me what I had to do:
'There are people who are more important to you than others. There are situations you have experienced, dreamed and desired which are more important to you than others. There are places you have actually been to, or visited in your imagination, that are more important to you than others. Begin with a situation that is a combination of a known face and a precise action in a precise place. Let that world come to life. Follow it. Live it. There are no rules. Everything can change along the way. Perhaps it all seems like a daydream, or a deep dream. Perhaps it's something you remember. Take all the time you want'" (Schino 2009: 230-231). The individual dream opens the door to the collective dream shared by the whole human race, for: "The dream is a universe. Man lives only in two universes which he calls 'reality' and 'dream'. […] in the universe of dream, the physical universe is not regarded in its linear development, but *simultaneously*. […] in the world of dream, history is like a movie: you can wind it back, you can put a stop to it; you can see *everything*, if you look attentively – you can even see how an insect excretes. Moreover, you can *empathize* with the insect, *feel* how it excretes" (Culianu 2010: 164). In *Andersen's Dream*, 2004, Barba suggests his actors *to create a universe which allows them to reflect upon their own obsessions, opinions and dreams, as well as mirror them*

(Wethal 2018: 223). To conceive this universe, *he asks each actor to prepare 'individual material' with a dramaturgical structure and to direct one of Andersen's fairy tales with colleagues as actors* (Wethal 2018: 223-224).

Again and again, Eugenio Barba changes the *hows* of creating his dramaturgy as *the years have taught him how important it is to redefine for himself the habitual working terms in order to distil new images, flavours and fragrances. It is as though he was being suffocated by the craft. The only way to breathe a little oxygen is continually to ask himself what theatre is; why he keeps on doing it; how to achieve a knowledge that contains its opposite, or in other words how to escape from the accumulation of experience which crystallises an identity, involuntarily becoming a barrier* (Barba 2002c: 4).

In *The Practitioner-Playwright* (2005) and in *Homo Felix Experiment: A Study of Shakespeare* (2005), reflecting on the dramaturgy of William Shakespeare, Molière, Carlo Gozzi, Carlo Goldoni, Alfred Jarry, Bertolt Brecht, Eugène Ionesco, Samuel Beckett, I asked myself what will happen with the exceptional dramaturgy *written on stage and not on page*. In this respect, Eugenio Barba's remark is relevant: *The writers wrote for the actors. Only when it was incarnated by the actors, the written text sprang from page to life. Today, we like it or not, the dramatic literature is no longer the spine of the theatre practice. Does this mean that the theatre life no longer has a long-lasting breath? Does this mean that its memory has become short? A few years ago, Richard Schechner considered this risk. He spoke about the new theatre civilisation, where the performance is written on stage, and not on page, as being a civilisation which risks to lose its memory* (Barba 2012a: 202). Indeed, the dramaturgy is not to be written and *read*, but to be *performed*. William Shakespeare *wrote* his plays not to be published, but to be *performed*.

The performance may be written on page or may be written on stage. It is up to us.

Quick reflections

Alfred Jarry's *King Ubu* has a huge impact on the twentieth century theatre. But Jarry is not alone. Antonin Artaud follows him closely. The Artaudian vision influences the researches of outstanding theatre practitioners.

The *psychological-realism* coexists with the *poetry in space*.

While the *representational theatre* slowly diminishes its power of attraction, *the poor theatre of the actor's technique* opens the door to new explorations.

From *pretext* to *context*.

The emphasis is no longer on gesture but on action.

The actors' physical-vocal actions are carriers of meanings and their incantation and dance reveal the co-existences of opposites: sacredness and blasphemy, sublimity and sordidness.

In the second half of the twentieth century, sometimes to make theatre is to set out on a *journey into the mankind's dream*.

For Eugène Ionesco and Samuel Beckett, the language of the theatre is the language of the ineffable, of *the inner self*.

Sometimes ignored, sometimes publicly idolised, the artist expands the frontiers of his creative freedom in an attempt to fully express his thoughts and ideas. It is as if his thoughts, piercing the walls of his mind prison, make him feel free. It reminds me both of Camus's concept of inner freedom developed in his novel *The Stranger* and of the freedom of the spirit that cannot be shadowed by the darkness of the outer. Generally speaking, through his work, an artist aims to reveal the nature of the relationship between the individual and his self and between the individual and society. A society which, at times, causes him to say: *I believe in a law of love, and I believe that the laws of love could be sufficient to organise human life in a beautiful and meaningful way without punishment and harm, and I also believe that as long as I can say these words, I live in a free land* (Biner 1972: 80).

Books, paintings and musical compositions may be preserved for centuries. Sometimes, the fate of a creation is to be forgotten, ignored or misinterpreted and rediscovered after long periods. It is the case of William Shakespeare's plays which enjoy their fame today due to August Schlegel's *act of restitution*. Or it is the case of Eugène Ionesco's plays, even today enigmas waiting to be solved, considered by some theatre practitioners out of fashion. In this regard, Jung's observation is relevant: "we have often found that a poet who has gone out of fashion is suddenly rediscovered. This happens when our conscious development has reached a higher level from which the poet can tell us something new. It was always present in his work but was hidden in a symbol, and only a renewal of the spirit of the time permits us to read its meaning. It needed to be looked at with fresher eyes, for the old ones could see in it only what they were accustomed to see" (Jung 1971: 101). So, the books, transcending eras, are capable of producing enchantment in their readers over centuries. The same enchantment one feels for instance when he discovers, after some time, something new in the book of a favourite writer. The theatre performance, an ephemeral act, which takes place *here and now*, might be enjoyed by the spectator or not. It might be remembered or not. If the spectator does not feel enchantment or does not have a revelation it is as if the performance dies in dunes of sand failing to provoke an extraordinary and unrepeatable experience. But when the spectator feels that he participates in a unique event, he lives an experience which *overturns* his habitual ways of perceiving and understanding reality and becomes eager to change himself. Eager to change his present through a different interpretation of his past and a different projection of his future. Only if the individual changes himself can he change the others. Utopia or possible reality? However, the artist does not adapt to the others' thinking and behavioural patterns, but helps them to see new possibilities of living their life.

    The theatre masters pursue their dreams: *Grotowski represents the pole of inner value and the tendency to shy away from artistic creation. Barba is the pole representing the existential and political value of the theatre, for both the actor and the spectator. He also represents the possibility that the time of the performance – and not just the time devoted to the theatre – might become a moment and a place of knowledge. The two different ways of conceiving the theatre by two great directors are perceived as, and 'have become', the two living poles of a single and specific way of conceiving and living the theatre.* (Schino 2009: 89)

Barba's *time for the performance* is the time for his reflections on dramaturgy. It is the time of the dramaturgy.

Performances dreamed with eyes wide open

Texts written about performances may, in the same way as plays, inspire visions of performances dreamed with eyes wide open by those who let themselves be carried along by the fascinating images generated by the meanings of the texts.

Ideas from the programme for *Ornitofilene* reverberate in *The Chronic Life* as, for instance, one of a human being's primary ways of manifesting himself is war both with himself and with the other. The idea of life as a permanent state of war is unveiled by Barba when he refers to the name and mission of his theatre: "A theatre cannot justify its existence if it is not conscious of its social mission. The adjective 'social' implies an emotional and ethical attitude towards others and the artistic result is always influenced by this attitude. The name of our theatre is not fortuitous. It seems natural to us to adopt the name of that force which has left its mark on our century: Odin, the god of war, the great 'berserk'. In the same way that our forbears evoked and struggled against demons, giving them free rein in collective ceremonies, all of us are gathered here – actors and spectators – to bring into the light the 'Odin' which lies in ambush in our darkness, and to fight it" (Barba-D'Urso 2000: 12).

Ornitofilene (*The Bird Lovers*), October 1965, is the first Odin Teatret's production. It was created in Oslo, based on a text by Jens Bjørneboe, adapted and directed by Eugenio Barba, played in the Norwegian language. Here, Barba alludes to an idea which most times, if not always, we choose to turn our back on: "One could say that he who tortures, mutilates his own humanity. The moment you strike someone else, you are killing the human being within yourself" (Nagel Rasmussen 2018: 39).

The theme of the performance is the progress which requires sacrifice.

At the same time it refers to the relationship between executioner and victim.

Place of action: a village in southern Italy. Time of action: "in the early sixties, those 'glorious years' of the economic boom" (Barba 1999b: 292). The executioners: former Nazi occupiers of the village. The victims: poor and savage Italians who hunt birds to cook and eat them. The story begins with "one of the local leaders who recognises, amongst a group of wealthy German tourists, some of the Nazi occupiers who had once oppressed, tortured and killed many of the villagers" (Barba 1999b: 292). The Germans, looking rich and pacifist, bargain with the villagers declaring: "You must stop your hunting. We will build a tourist paradise here in your village. You will be well-off. But no civilised foreigner will want to come to a place where there is so much useless killing" (Barba 1999b: 292). On the surface, the progress consists in the transition from a *barbarian paradise* to a "tourist paradise" (Barba 1999b: 292), from primitivism to civilisation.

Reflecting on the story of the performance, a few questions come to my mind: Can someone who was victimised be capable of forgiveness? Forgetfulness? Capable of going on with his life when he is forced to accept a past full of horrors, tortures, abominable crimes? Is poverty a burden so heavy that succeeds in making the victim reach out to his aggressor? Do the loss of dignity and the compromise lead to real progress? Must yesterday's enemy be today's friend?

What kind of progress do we speak about? That of a village covered with a blooded veil and whose villagers prepare themselves to embellish it with coins? Can terrible wounds be healed with money? And if the answer is yes, another question arises: what are memories for?

However, the villagers are so poor that they accept their former Nazi occupiers' proposal. And then something unexpected happens. A young girl takes her own life. If in the original text her father, played by Torgeir Wethal, commits suicide, in Barba's performance, the girl, played by Else Marie Laukvik, sacrifices herself. Her act reveals the terrible "idea that time makes people softer and that, in the end, it is the children – in this case, the daughter – who end up paying for their parents' loss of ideals" (Nagel Rasmussen 2018: 38).

I imagine that the innocent young would have fought with their former executioners with bare hands for their freedom. The young girl, not capable of accepting the *new order* as she lives in a *natural order*, sees in death a liberating, blessing act. At the same time, I imagine the older men of the village saying: *Those who are young still have time to grow old and enjoy the fruits of progress! We do not have this time! Therefore we choose the progress now*. Obviously, in this case, one can think no longer of honour and dignity.

Just before putting an end to her life, the young girl murmurs: "'Those who loved me have abandoned me. Now I shall see how alone one is in death.' Her father laughs mockingly and, turning to the spectators, announces: 'Your children!'" (Barba 1999b: 292)

Your children, your future! Dream on!

Kaspariana has its premiere in September 1967, in Holstebro. It is based on a text by Ole Sarvig, adapted and directed by Eugenio Barba, played by the actors in different Scandinavian languages. Beginning with this performance, the director devises the *sonorous dramaturgy*: "Exclamations and calls, whispers, muttering, shouts, groans, laughter, sudden silence, crystal clear or hoarse tones, phrases modulated as nursery rhymes, psalms or traditional songs, intonations as litanies or animal sounds – bleating, neighing, twittering – were the basis for our sonorous dramaturgy. And, above all, during a dramatic climax, singing replaced words" (Barba 2010a: 40).

A sonorous dramaturgy on *a sonorous island in the middle of a sonorous ocean* (Culianu 1992: 32).

Kaspariana unveils the story of an *innocent (or wild) boy* whose fate is sealed by a community that decides *to educate* him, to initiate him in becoming a *real man*. The young man is given a name: "Kaspar shall be your name" (Barba 1999b: 295). *The final stage of initiation is a struggle, and when the spectator's eye perceives Kaspar's hands and those of his opponent stretching out to grab a knife, the lights suddenly go out* (Barba 1999b: 294).

Barba conceives the scenic space as *space-river*, that is as the space of the spectator face to face with the other spectators. In this regard, I think that Martin Berg's comment after one performance is relevant: "And there, behind all this, are the faces of the other spectators opposite me, looking into my face as I look into theirs, and the eyes I see before me are so moved that I believe I understand what they see" (Barba 1999b: 294).

After 43 years, during the rehearsals for *The Chronic Life*, held in the Blue Room, Torgeir Wethal *presents a scene from Kaspariana, with faint sounds and a rare, delicate transparency* (Nagel Rasmussen 2011: 78), reviving one of his past scenic experiences: initiation as *melete thanatos*.

The suspended future!

Ferai, June 1969, based on a text by Peter Seeberg, adapted and directed by Eugenio Barba, interpreted in the Scandinavian languages of the actors, tells the story of *a young man who wins both power and the daughter of the dead king as his bride* (Barba 1999b: 296). It seems that *the unity and conflict of opposites* in the story are penetrated by the profound connotations of *eros and thanatos, struggle and power, on the one hand, love and sensuality, on the other hand* (Nagel Rasmussen 2018: 73). The transition from tyranny to enlightened absolutism, from total despotism to despotism with a human face, from slavery to fake freedom, from the punishment of those found guilty of crimes to their treatment as patients becomes noticeable. The executioner-victim relationship is replaced by the doctor-patient relationship. "The performance begins where *Kaspariana* finished: with a struggle for the possession of a knife", but now *the young man fights with his bare hands and exhibits another kind of violence: a smile upon his lips, not violent like a ferocious dog but with a feline gentleness, harmonious, acrobatic, dancing, and revealing implacability only at the precise moment of the strike* (Barba 1999b: 296). When his bride commits suicide, the young king, *after mourning her briefly, tramples on her mortal remains* (Barba 1999b: 296). Alas, there is such perfidy, so much arrogance and cold-bloodedness of the new tyrant who grins superiorly. It is as if I hear the burst of a cosmic laughter aware that nothing ever changes.

The future of violence! Or the future of the individual who snarls behind his social mask. After all, "We are all equal in this hour of democracy" (Barba 1999b: 297).

Torgeir Wethal, in *Frammenti del mondo di un attore*, reveals to us important aspects of Barba's working process: "In the traditional sense of the term, I have never *acted* a part in an Odin Teatret performance. Most of our performances did *not* arise from the interpretation of written texts, but were the result of long and particular working processes. The starting points for these processes were concrete and exacting themes. Themes that had emotional and historical parallels with us and with our time. Both the 'characters' and the story of the performance grow slowly during the course of our meeting/dialogue with the theme. A world is slowly constructed. I live in this world. [...] In the meeting with each new performance, I have always needed to try and discover sides of myself and models of behaviour that are more concealed than those I usually show in everyday life" (Schino 2009: 229).

If Barba had not worked, in his early productions, on devising his *sonorous dramaturgy* and *dramaturgy of the space*, if he had not investigated certain existential themes such as initiation, sacrifice, suicide, progress and *themes that had emotional and historical parallels with the actors* (Schino 2009: 229), *if the actors had not become a part of his creative being* (Nagel Rasmussen 2018: 88), he would not have been thoroughly prepared to develop his personal way of creating dramaturgy. *My Father's House*, premiered in April 1972, is *an intricate web of contradictions, a dance of paradoxes* (Nagel Rasmussen 2018: 89). The director-playwright creates the story of the performance through improvisations. During the process of building the characters, he lets himself be inspired by his inner images, the fruits of his imagination. The strange and profound images contain an idea which Barba has explored in his previous performances, that is: "The human being is a cruel animal. Whatever goodness is to be found is just an exception" (Nagel Rasmussen 2018: 92).

This time Dostoevsky's life and works are the source of the performance corroborated with the director's 'ghosts' imbued with his countless sub-texts (Nagel Rasmussen 2018: 92). *My Father's House* is the performance which reminds Tony D'Urso of "the Tarantolata rituals in Salento" (Barba-D'Urso 2000: 9), rituals of exorcism, in which the person bitten by the tarantula spider and consequently possessed by it, dances on the dizzying rhythms of the music hoping to be healed.

Youth without age and life without death

For Eugenio Barba, the Parcae predicted *youth without age and life without death*.

When I first read *On Directing and Dramaturgy: Burning the House*, I was amazed to discover the playwright-practitioner's way of *writing his play on stage* shrouded in the mists of time. Barba's dramaturgy reminded me of Molière's and William Shakespeare's process of creating their dramatic texts on stage. I was already deeply impressed by his study *Actions at Work* published in *The Secret Art of the Performer: A Dictionary of Theatre Anthropology*, by his unique perspective of *seeing* dramaturgy as *the work of the actions* in which the minutest spectacular element is *action*. His dramaturgy, a *plurality of dramaturgies*, namely the *dramaturgy of the actor*, the *narrative dramaturgy* and the *evocative dramaturgy,* is the fruit of long years of research and remarkable professional experiences. Due to his outstanding work, Eugenio Barba is considered one of the greatest theatre reformers of the second half of the twentieth century and the beginning of the twenty-first century.

"A performance, too, can give the experience of a space-time in which the 'after' can precede the 'before'. A conditioned reflex makes us associate the connections between a 'before' and an 'after' with those of cause and effect. The fact that one event follows another doesn't mean that the latter is the result of the former. When in my work I stressed the links based on simultaneity, I tried to oppose the spectators' tendency and need to recognise the relationships of cause and effect in the evident concatenation of the actions in time." (Barba 2010a: 106) Eugenio Barba challenges us *overturning* the equation cause/past – effect/present. If we have been taught that the individual usually thinks that what happens today is undoubtedly the effect of what happened yesterday, Barba's performances make us meditate on the idea that our dreams and illusions of the future shape our present. As *time past is perhaps contained in time present* often shaping a predictable future, so *time future is perhaps contained in time present* (T. S. Eliot) often shaping a different past. Unfortunately, haunted by memories of the past or projections of the future, we live in the past or in the future and never in the present. At night, in our dreams, we listen to the mermaid's song telling us who we were or foretelling who we shall be. It is useless to dream of *another* time past or *another* time future when we do not live in the present.

Barba spins the thread of his *narrative dramaturgy* as if he spins the thread of human destiny. Verses about being naive, lullabies, child's whispers, love songs, wails, incantations reverberate into his *space-river*. After his performance *My Father's House*, he definitively renounces to create a performance based on a preexisting text. Accordingly, he sets out on a hunt for documentation of his performance. When the hunt is over, his game bag is crammed with poems, novels, enigmas. Then he weaves the dramaturgical threads so that the scenic confrontation takes place both on the worldly chessboard and the individual's chessboard where the bishop / the unconscious fights with the pawn / the common sense, the knight / the imagination measures its strength with the rook / the reason. He creates a strange chessboard-stage where the blue light reveals its metaphysical dimension and archetypal experiences and dreams come to life. Where between dream and reality sometimes there is a second, sometimes an eternity. The never-ending second of a never-dying story. I imagine his *dramaturgy of the actor* as an incarnation of the actor's *scenic self*. As the actor lives many lives in one life it is as if his scenic self contains both the history of human experiences and his personal history. Or it is as if the actor, throwing off his chameleon scenic cloak, reveals a complex mechanism resembling Dali's melting clock. *A soft clock which is a meditation on his character and his own life.* I suppose that during the process of visualising his character, the actor immerses into his scenic self, into the universe of his interior, and there he becomes fully aware that not only his "thought proceeds by leaps, connecting the past with the fantasies about the future and blending planes and dimensions which don't respect a chronological or logical succession" (Barba 2010a: 107) but also the thought of his character. So he creates both the outer life and inner life of his character accordingly.

How can we live and have no story to tell? (Dostoevsky) Living or in the past or in the future, never in the present, afraid of losing our ego and certitudes, we have become cold-minded and emotionless. Suffocating our inner child, forgetting to breathe the air of freedom, to live fully, we suffer of loneliness and depression. We do the same things each day, think the same thoughts each evening, dream the same dream each night. We have distanced from ourselves and play the role society has given us. We are not happy. We do not feel the joy of being one with our secret life the way we used to feel when we were children. We lost our hope that we can live our life *differently* and *totally*. It is true that we have no story to tell. So, we dream our story wishing to become true. We dream about being heroes even though we know so well there are no heroes. We dream of serendipity. And we are excited when looking for a needle we find a beetle. Do we have our own story only if we have the chance *to meet* others who in turn have their stories because they have the chance *to meet* us? Eugenio Barba's dramaturgy does not tell a *single* story. Behind every action, a story is concealed. In his dramaturgy, he spins many stories emerged from his *wound-necessity*, preoccupations and questions.

What if we burn the sick house we live in and take from there *a coin* which, hiding in our fist, we always carry with us? What if one day, rummaging in every corner of our inner world to search for the truth of our soul buried in the dust, we see the minuscule grains of powder glowing with light? What if we free ourselves from our prejudices which incessantly devour us? What if we look like children look at the fire to see beyond what is obvious? What if we set our life on fire and start all over again? What if we enter the living Dramaturgy of Eugenio Barba?

(The text was first published in *Contemporanul – Ideea Europeană*, No 12, Bucharest, 2012, p. 37)

The dramaturgy of a spectator

Is the spectator the key?

Is it possible to speak about the dramaturgy of the spectator?
"It is strange to speak about 'dramaturgy of the spectator', and often I have been reproached that this expression is meaningless. I have stubbornly maintained it. It helped me to point out my main effort: to create a performance which could assume a shared sense and at the same time might whisper a different confidence to every spectator. And which appeared diverse every time they watched it." (Barba 2010a: 13)

The *evocative dramaturgy* is Barba's most uncommon level of organising his dramaturgy. When the director speaks about "The evocative dimension – the level enabling the performance and its spectators to go beyond their own limits" (Barba 2010a: 183), he makes reference to the "dramaturgy of the spectator" which is revealed to us from the perspective of the relationship that the director-playwright has as *first spectator* (Barba 2010a: 184) with his *spectators-fetishes*. However, during a performance, each spectator has his own experience that does not let itself be shared. While he stays seated watching the performance, which is usually the case at almost all performances, he constantly reacts. Many times, what is visible is that he smiles or laughs or claps his hands. But sometimes it happens that a certain performance impresses him so strongly that it takes him back instantly to a place or a moment dear to him or makes him dream with his eyes open of his secret wishes. Then the thoughts he thinks and the emotions he has are linked somehow to the idea that the performance addresses him directly, that an intimate bond has been established between them. Often, after such a performance, the spectator feels an impulsive need to tell others about it, to relive his reactions, *to recall it with the same personal implications and the same degree of ambiguity with which he lives the dramatic events of daily life* (Barba 2010a: 25). When he does this, sometimes he makes use of concatenation and other times compresses many images, actions, micro-scenes into a few words trying to create the impression of simultaneity. For instance, when I tried to describe a few simultaneous images and actions that I glimpsed during one of the rehearsals for *The Chronic Life*, my *oral story* went like this: *And, all of a sudden, I saw at the same time a patch of blue sky, welding metal fire sparks, angel wings melted by the heat of the sun, trembling hands desperately stretching to grab the bait put on a hook, a rain of coins falling on the floor, and all this while I was dreaming with eyes wide open how I feverishly smell a red rose that I delicately hold in my hands.*

However, a spectator recalls a certain performance only if it has left deep traces on the skin of his heart. Only if the director has succeeded to make him "step into the torrid zone of that *art of memory which is theatre*" (Barba 2010a: 176). It is only then that the performance may come back to his memory with such power that he feels the strange sensation that it inhabits his present.

We know

We know that a performance has the capacity to captivate the spectators and sometimes to change their lives.

Jerzy Grotowski makes the distinction between spectator and audience underlining the idea that his performances address each spectator and not a mass of spectators. It is the spectator who might be fascinated by the "profound images" (Schino 2009: 72) of a performance. It is the spectator, and not the audience, who is likely to experience dilation of his senses, a *change of state*.

But who is the spectator to whom a theatre performance addresses today? Why does he go to the theatre? Is he the person eager to share with his lover a special moment celebrated afterwards with champagne at a romantic dinner? Is he the one given to intellectual pleasures? Or the one with cultural aspirations? Or the one who, night after night, is present at all the sophisticated events, afraid not to miss the most sophisticated one? Is he a friend or supporter of the actors? Or the one who never misses a certain performance because it is played by great actors or made by great directors? Or the one who has never been at the theatre and naively asks: "What is theatre?". Or the one who chooses the performance according to the name of the playwright or the title of the play or the company's prestige? Or the one whose job it is to see a performance and comment on it in terms of aesthetic criteria?

Is he/she the one who wishes to feel excitement? Or the one who wants to have an extraordinary experience? Or the one who dreams of being offered a journey to self-revelation? Or the one who considers the performance a means to bring about social and political emancipation? Is he/she a theatre lover?

So, why does someone go to the theatre? To participate in an unforgettable event? To entertain himself? Or going to the theatre in most cases is the result of family and school education? Or is it something that, from time to time, should be done? Between YouTube, Facebook, LinkedIn and Twitter, who knows, once, maybe, twice a year, one may choose to see a theatre performance as well.

And then to whom do the directors and actors address themselves? To whom?

Nowadays, whether we want it or not, the rhythm of our life is more and more frantic and many times, after a day's work, we feel too tired to go to the theatre or cinema. The TV is next to the bed or armchair and with a simple touch of the remote control we have access to hundreds of channels. Our laptops are perpetually turned on in our homes and when we go to bed we take our smartphone with us. So, we take pleasure, for a few hours a day, in watching videos on YouTube, liking or commenting on Facebook or LinkedIn posts. Irresistibly attracted to virtual worlds, often we evade reality. In this context, a theatre performance might seem boring or uninteresting.

And then why does the spectator go to the theatre? In 1908, Craig remarks: "Ask them the reason why they have come to the theatre. Five reply, 'I come to see Mr. —- act.' Three reply, 'It is such a great play, I like to hear it so much.' Two giggle and reply, 'We don't know why we come, but we think it is such fun.' Two are there from a sense of duty both to the actors of the play and to the audience; and the other eight will give us several elaborate and conflicting reasons for their presence. One will say, that it is the extraordinary sense of the impossible, the grim absurdity of the whole thing, which fascinates him. (Excellent judge!) The second will tell you that, after having spent the day among dull and matter-of-fact people, it is quite interesting to find a body of people who will sit still while actors and scenery are pretending on the stage. Then there is the third – the critical man [...] – this man will be there, because somehow he feels that the thing would be incomplete without him; he is one of the men who knows – has he not read all about it? Then next to him is sitting a young lady, who, with the intelligence which is natural in her sex, is ready to see *all* that is there and more (or less), if required. [...] Next to her sits the grumbler, one who goes to a theatre because he must, and who, I believe, is always the one who is most deeply moved by what he sees. Yet when the curtain is once down he will tell you that was not the way to do it at all" (Craig 1957: 113-114).

Anyway, in the third millennium, no matter what reasons we might have to go to the theatre, one thing is certain: once we are seated, we begin to wait, thrilled with expectations, for the performance to begin. After all, we have paid the ticket price in exchange for the product.

A performance is built during rehearsals and reaches its climax when it is shared with its spectators. In every representation, a re-creation of a past experience, the actor does not reiterate his score, but re-creates it in *the present of the performance*. Similar to a child's play, the actor's play has to be convincing. When Barba speaks about *the effect of organicity*, he refers to "[the actor's] capacity of making the spectator experience a body-in-life. The main task of an actor is not to be organic, but to create the perception of organicity to the eyes and senses of the spectator" (Barba 2012a: 129). The *effect of organicity* occurs when the actor *goes beyond technique and hypnotises the spectators with the fervour of his emotions* (Panigrahi 1996: 89). In this respect, Anna Pavlova's unearthly dance in *the dying swan* springs to my mind. At the same time, a performance may produce in the spectator sometimes catharsis, sometimes revelation, sometimes seconds of ecstasy and sometimes all of these. The spectator is in need of catharsis for he longs to purify his inner life as well as of revelation. Ergo, he gets into the *carriage of the performance which takes him* to unknown realms where he has the possibility of living an experience likely to change his life.

Even if only a bit of it. A bit as big as a cosmos.

But of which spectators am I speaking? (Barba 2010a: 183)

After the tremendous international success Barba has with his third performance, *Ferai*, in Paris at the *Théâtre des Nations* and in Venice at the Biennale, in 1969, it becomes clear for him that "in theatre there is a form of sensorial and emotional communication that determines the spectator's feelings and perception – an almost biological, sensual relationship" (Nagel Rasmussen 2018: 74). His studies on the condition of the spectator lead him to identify *the different natures of the spectator*. In *On Directing and Dramaturgy: Burning the House*, he makes reference to his *spectators-fetishes who reflect the diverse ways in which a performance is alive* (Barba 2010a: 184): "These spectators-fetishes were a few concrete people, with recognisable characteristics: a child carried away by the euphoria of rhythm and wonder, but unable to appraise symbols, metaphors and artistic originality; Knudsen, an old skilled carpenter, who knew how to value small details; the spectator who thought he did not understand, but danced sitting on his seat; a friend of mine who had seen many of my performances, and lived again the pleasure of recognising what made him love them [...]; the blind Jorge Luis Borges, who enjoyed the least literary allusions and the thick layers of vocal information; the deaf Beethoven listening to the performance through his eyes, appreciating the symphony of its physical actions; a bororo from Amazonia who envisaged it as a ceremony for the forces of nature; a person I loved and whom I would like to be proud of me and my actors" (Barba 2010a: 184). So, here is the child with his amazing capacity of concocting a story in a blink and totally believe in it: "Let's pretend the glass has got soft like gauze, so that we can get through. Why, it's turning into a sort of mist now I declare! It'll be easy enough to get through" (Carroll 2016: 9); or pretending to fly on a broom on full moon; or being entirely convinced that he is a charming prince the moment he puts a rainbow coloured paper crown on his head. Like the actor, he enjoys playing. So, often it may happen that he sings or drums on pots or dances screaming with laughter one moment and cries the next moment and then, all of a sudden, he sings and dances again. Cheerful and tireless, the child has an inborn tendency to love to play.

Perhaps that is why he is the theatre reformers' favourite spectator. Or perhaps because he does not mask his reactions or play the role of the civilised spectator. The truth is that he has no interest in hiding his thoughts and emotions. So, if he is bored, he does not conceal his boredom, if he rejoices, he truly laughs. The child, like Shakespeare's wise fool, is free to *speak out the truth he thinks*.

"The theatre's raw material is not the actor, nor the space, nor the text, but the attention, the seeing, the hearing, the mind of the spectator. Theatre is the art of the spectator." (Barba 1996b: 31) Barba investigates the nature of his *spectators-fetishes decomposing their reactions and mental behaviours into a few possible basic attitudes, mixing and attuning them the same way he does with the actions of the actors* (Barba 2010a: 184). Expanding the architecture of his vision, the director designs a room for the spectator into the house of the performance as *each spectator who might have watched his performance is considered an individual made up of a blend of his spectators-fetishes* (Barba 2010a: 184).

In *Angelanimal: Lost Techniques for the Spectator*, Barba evokes the time when "theatre was the celebration of perturbation and excitement. The actors addressed the animal and the angel in the spectators, goading that part of their reptilian brain in which the instincts of hunger, fear, sexuality and faith nestle" (Barba 2006: 2). Undeniably, through his dramaturgy, the director addresses *the angel and animal in the spectator*. In this regard, Barba tells us: "Angelanimal is the name of a spectator. Or better, my way of naming a facet of the complex set of intellectual, emotional, critical, rational and instinctive reactions that compose the collective noun 'spectator'. It is the name that I give to the animal hiding in the depth of my brain as well as to the indissoluble angel that hovers as a shadow in the empty space above or under it. People of science could perhaps attribute to Angelanimal a precise abode in the macrocosm of our skull, between the reptilian and the limbic brain" (Barba 2006: 3). Victor Turner, referring to the reptilian brain and the limbic brain as being closely linked to the ritual, reminds of d'Aquili's and Laughlin's model "'according to which the minor or non-dominant hemisphere (usually the right hemisphere) is identified with the trophotropic or baseline energy state system, and the dominant or major hemisphere (usually the left) that governs analytical verbal and causal thinking is identified with the ergotropic or energy-expending system", suggesting that: "when either the ergotropic or trophotropic system is hyperstimulated, there results a 'spillover' into the opposite system after 'three stages of tuning', often by 'driving behavior' employed to facilitate ritual trance. [...] when the left hemisphere is stimulated beyond a certain threshold, the right hemisphere is also stimulated. [...] the rhythmic activity of ritual, aided by sonic, visual, photic, and other kinds of 'driving', may lead in time to simultaneous maximal stimulation of both systems, causing ritual participants to experience what the authors call 'positive, ineffable affect'" (Turner 1988: 165). For me, *The Chronic Life,* at every rehearsal, has functioned *as a ritual* (Barba-D'Urso 2000: 244). *Watching the stories of fictitious characters and, at the same time, gliding into a world of my own,* The Chronic Life *not only has succeeded in whispering a secret to me, a premonition or a question, but also in evoking another reality. The performance has never been an appearance, but an apparition visiting my inner city* (Barba 2010a: 183).

About *The Chronic Life* in the programme for the performance:

Text: Ursula Andkjær Olsen and Odin Teatret – Actors: Kai Bredholt, Roberta Carreri, Jan Ferslev, Elena Floris, Donald Kitt, Tage Larsen, Sofia Monsalve, Iben Nagel Rasmussen, Fausto Pro, Julia Varley – Dramaturg: Thomas Bredsdorff – Literary Adviser: Nando Taviani – Lighting Design: Odin Teatret – Lighting Adviser: Jesper Kongshaug – Scenic Space: Odin Teatret – Scenic Space Advisers: Jan de Neergaard, Antonella Diana – Music: Traditional and contemporary melodies – Costumes: Odin Teatret, Jan de Neergaard – Drawings: Giulia Capodieci – Cover: Peter Bysted – Technical Director: Fausto Pro – Director Assistants: Raúl Iaiza, Pierangelo Pompa, Ana Woolf – Director and Dramaturgy: Eugenio Barba.

Production: Nordisk Teaterlaboratorium (Holstebro), Teatro de La Abadia (Madrid), The Grotowski Institute (Wrocław).

First performance: 12 September 2011 in Holstebro.

    Characters:
    – a Black Madonna
    – the widow of a Basque officer

- a Chechnyan refugee
- a Rumanian housewife
- a Danish lawyer
- a rock musician from the Faroe Islands
- a Colombian boy searching for his father disappeared in Europe
- an Italian street violinist
- two mercenaries

"The action of the performance takes place simultaneously in different countries of Europe in 2031, after the third civil war.

Individuals and groups with different backgrounds come together and challenge each other driven by uprooting, war, unemployment and financial crises. What happens when newcomers want to implant themselves on foreign soil and be part of a society that thinks it has solid cultural roots? What misunderstandings and discoveries arise from this confrontation? How do people live in a country at war in which soldiers become visible only when they return from afar in coffins?

A boy arrives from Latin America to the feverish carnival of the civilised regions of Europe. He is searching for his father who has inexplicably disappeared. Little more than a child, he ignores what everybody knows: that life is a chronic disease from which our planet with its history is unable to free itself. Everybody knows that a thousand doors lead to freedom, and everybody nourishes this knowledge by eating without hunger and drinking without thirst. Everybody knows that they have a great past, and from this greatness each cuts out his own shred of honour and identity. They answer the foreign boy's questions, teaching him to avoid that worst of all vices – Hope. 'Stop searching for your father' they whisper, while escorting him from one door to another among the wreckage of fables that they call their history.

It is neither knowledge nor innocence that saves the boy. A new ignorance helps him to discover his door. Amid the bewilderment of all of us who no longer believe in the unbelievable: that just one victim is worth more than any value. More than God."

Eyewitnessing

... my emotive and intellectual responses ...
(Marinis 1987: 101) to *The Chronic Life*

(Text written during the rehearsals for *The Chronic Life*, September-October 2010 and February-March 2011, and completed in 2013)

Wednesday, 29 September 2010, Holstebro

Eugenio Barba whispers to his actors

As in a dream, I rush towards the left side of the White Room and take a seat in the third row of spectators. I feel a knot in my stomach. My body shivers. And my palms sweat. Not being capable of controlling my emotions, I put my glasses on and begin to write my diary:

In the centre of the stage: a long table, covered in a white sheet. Is it a sacrifice table? A bed? A coffin?
 At one end of the stage: a wooden wall.
 The strange-looking hooks of various sizes, seemingly splashed with blood, make me think of an infernal place.
 The first scene: the Puppet (the Puppet will be referred to as 'he' and not 'it') of human size sits at the table. His huge, empty eyes look kind and sad. I sense his pain. I see resignation in his gaze. And I start thinking about the mystery of the Puppet. What does he symbolise? *Is he the symbol of man in a magical and religious ritual? Does he take part in a celebration in praise of the Creation* (Craig 1957: 91-92)? *Does he play a decisive role in an act of exorcising the evil spirits?* Is he the *symbol of human being lacked of his own consistency that listen to any external impulsion* (Chevalier-Gheerbrant 1995: 270)? In the epic *Mahabharata*, it is said that *man's gestures are manipulated by another like those of a wooden puppet on strings* (Chevalier-Gheerbrant 1995: 271). Does he have something in common with Pinocchio? I do not know. Lolito, this

is the name of the Puppet. In a previous performance, *The Land of Nod*, he was "a naughty and mocking guardian angel" (Nagel Rasmussen 2011: 76); now he is a quiet boy dressed in a school uniform who probably waits for someone to smile at him. For Iben Nagel Rasmussen, who plays the Black Madonna, the Puppet *becomes the Christ, a corpse, a wounded man whom she drags along, raises above her head, embraces on her knees as a 'Pietà' or throws over her shoulder as a bundle* (Nagel Rasmussen 2011: 76).

The wound is omnipresent: all actors limp. My senses sharpen while being totally engrossed in the micro-scenes. So, here is Kai Bredholt, who plays the Widow of a Basque Officer, animating the Puppet as "the poet who gives life and personality to scissors, flowers, piggybanks, toys and things from the world of children" (Bredholt 2004: 19). Iben Nagel Rasmussen's wielding of the sword, which I later find out is a replica of a samurai sword, evokes the goddess Kali's rotating arms. Roberta Carreri, who will play the Rumanian Housewife, behaves like a woman who cleans the house only to forget memories that hurt. The scenic space seems to be inhabited by shadows that limp ceaselessly. Spectral apparitions emerged from a dark and misty realm. Why do they limp? What does their limp mean? Infirmity? Unbalance? Loss of a loved one? Unending distress? Jacob's wrestling with the Angel? Oedipus' wound? Hephaestus' limping? Near the wooden wall hurt by hooks, in the space called the *storeroom,* the actors look like they are haunted by premonitions. While I try to detect the tiniest movements of the actors in a seeming stillness, the daily ritual that Winnie, half-buried in her *sid,* performs in Samuel Beckett's *Happy Days* comes to my mind.

I catch sight of Donald Kitt who plays a Mercenary: wearing a black mask on his face, almost completely engulfed in a reddish and yellowish blanket, he looks feeble in the wheelchair; a ridiculous figure lost in a sordid landscape. Tage Larsen, who plays the Danish Lawyer, and Julia Varley, who plays the Chechnyan Refugee, enter an attraction-rejection game. Jan Ferslev, who plays the Rock Musician from the Faroe Islands, whips the table, angrily. Fausto Pro, the other Mercenary, takes the Young Colombian, played by Sofia Monsalve, in his arms and puts him on a casket to connect his heart to electricity. Heartbeats and murmurs of a prayer are heard. The young boy's heart is disconnected, and his corpse is placed on the bed and covered in a white sheet. Simultaneous actions are performed: the Black Madonna drags the Puppet-corpse; the Chechnyan Refugee covers her eyes with cards; the Danish Lawyer gesticulates with a passport; the Rock Musician whips himself; the Rumanian Housewife, in her attempts to fly, breaks her angel wings and falls to the floor; the Young Colombian sings a sorrowful song; the Widow of a Basque Officer runs carrying a block of ice in her arms; a Mercenary nails an iron heart into the Black Madonna's chest; the other Mercenary brutally throws the musical instruments in a dustbin; the Italian Violinist, Elena Floris' character, plays the violin and gradually the sounds of music replace the noises of war.

A universe of sadness-loneliness, of the man-puppet, man-sick soul, man-connected / disconnected to / from a power source, man who faces imminent death, slowly comes into being. Each prop has its own story and is an organic prolongation of the actor. Many times, I spin a possible thread to link the scenes in an attempt to decipher the enigma of the performance, and I realise it does not tell a single story: there are the stories of the actors whose *secrets* are hidden behind their actions; then the stories of the actors' essentialized lines resembling riddles, of the relationships between actors, between actor and text, costume, prop, space, music, spectator. For brief moments, I have the impression that the actors' characters, breathing in a Chekhovian atmosphere, are marked by a subtle alienating behaviour, as their dialogues seem to be shaped into monologues.

Friday, 1 October 2010, Holstebro

Time retrieves its freedom and can glide forwards or backwards

(Barba 2010a: 107)

The dialogue between Alice and the White Queen comes to my mind:

"White Queen: 'That's the effect of living backwards. [...] It always makes one a little giddy at first. [...] But there is one great advantage in it, that one's memory works both ways.'

> Alice: 'I'm sure mine *only works one way*. I can't remember things before they happen.'
>
> White Queen: 'It's a poor sort of memory that only works backwards.'
>
> Alice: 'What sort of things do you remember best?'
>
> White Queen: 'Oh! ... Things that happened the week after next.'" (Carroll 2016: 45)

Ferdinando Taviani, in his *Presentazione* to Eugenio Barba's book, *La conquista della differenza: Trentanove paesaggi teatrali*, notices that, from the beginning of the performance, the director-playwright uses the device of *reversal*, for *as if nothing has happened* the Black Madonna *moves forward to one end of the stage, lies on the floor and raises her legs in the air*; from this moment, *time will be able to go back and forth, and the story will flow from the near future to the distant past abolishing any rational intertwining with the present* (Barba 2012a: IV). So, the Black Madonna *raises her legs in the air as if nothing has happened*, as if there has not pre-existed a particular cause to generate her action. It is a hilarious action in contrast to the solemn atmosphere created in the first scene. It is a sudden unexpected change, a quick shift from tragic to comic, an act of estrangement from oneself and others. The alienating device is also used in the scene of *the collective suicide* in which the actors, fallen to the ground, after they have swallowed drops of poison, slowly come back to life and then stare, each at his/her playing card, as if they read in it the next scene they are going to perform. Do the actors detach themselves from their own vision of death? Do they perform a ritual of initiation? Is it a spiritual rebirth? However, it seems that the Young Colombian goes through initiation. The scene *murder on the ship* is eloquent in this sense. After the boy is killed, the Black Madonna works a miracle: she cuts the sail with her sword and gently takes the Young Colombian out of the canvas. Alive for a second time, he starts to sing. A miracle also happens in the final scene when the dead boy rises again and comes out of the coffin.

The possible representations of the past and future in the present of the performance, the possible near-death experiences, the miracles, and the reversals are part of the director-playwright's vision. There are micro-sequences marked by acerbic criticism in which particular historical, religious, social, political, cultural aspects are treated with derision. Eugenio Barba's detachment from his personal experiences is also noticeable. It is as if one enters a time of 'buried in blood' historical facts interwoven with the director's life events. A time that seems to be projected by prophecy: a vision of a future world in agony.

Eternal moments in time and strange silences when I hear only the sound of the water drops that fall as rain.

Tuesday, 5 October 2010, Holstebro

Scenes are continuously subject to changes

Scene 1: *Let's remember*

A soldier's cap, that makes direct reference to war, hangs on a hook. The table seems to be veiled in bright white snow. The Puppet wears three-quarter trousers, a white shirt, a black wool vest, a scarf. The actors manipulate the Puppet trying out different positions such as: sitting down at the table, with his right hand on the table and his left hand raised, with hands clasped, with his back turned to the table, staring at the hooks as if he asks himself: why does death come for the one whose life has not ended yet? The Black Madonna, limping, gets near the Puppet, speaks to him, smiles to him, and prays for him. The Widow, dressed in *long black trousers that hide high heeled boots, a black blouse tied at the back, a pearl necklace and a black shawl fastened with a cameo, simple, symbolic jewellery worn by a woman with class* (Bredholt 2011: 29), carries in serviettes, plates, cutlery, glasses. After she talks to the Puppet, she places him in a corner of the performance space facing the spectators. At this moment, the Young Colombian makes his appearance. The Widow feeds the boy and clears the table. Then she puts the Puppet on the table-catafalque, covers him in a silvery sheet, and sings to him. During the Widow's song, the boy runs in circles with a block of ice in his arms. The Widow takes the block of ice and puts it under the Puppet's head. Then she washes the Puppet and passionately kisses him. At the end of the scene, the Widow and the Young Colombian leave the space singing.

Scene 2: *I wanna die easy when I die*

The Black Madonna whispers unintelligible words in a secret language; after that, carrying the corpse of the Puppet in her arms, she exits with light footsteps, barely touching the floor. At the same time, the Chechnyan Refugee enters. At first, she uses the cards as family photos, which she shows to the spectators, then improvises series of actions. Regarding her improvisation with the cards, Julia Varley tells us: "I improvise with the cards: I make them fly, I rub them, I use them to clean my hands, wash the floor, cover my eyes, I shuffle them, pick them up in different ways, I sow them as seeds, I build a labyrinth, I offer them, stick them on my tongue, hold them like a cigarette or a fan, I fold them, use them to play different rhythms, I let them caress and kiss, I climb on the pack as if it were the base of a monument, I cry and the cards fall from my eyes like tears ... I hang a card with a black ribbon like the photographs I have seen hanging round the necks of the Mothers of the Disappeared in Plaza de Mayo in Buenos Aires" (Varley 2011b: 45). The Rumanian Housewife hangs two broad, blue wings on the hooks, spreads colourful cloths and flowers on the table, cries out joyfully: "How beautiful they are! I want them!", sings *I wanna die easy when I die*, and greedily bites into a piece of bread. The Danish Lawyer enters the space holding a seven-branched lit candlestick. The Black Madonna reappears with the Puppet, this time, dressed in a soldier uniform. Simultaneous micro-sequences are performed: the Chechnyan Refugee builds a bridge out of cards, the Rumanian Housewife tries to suffocate herself with a plastic bag, the Black Madonna sings and plays with the Puppet. The scene climaxes with all the actors singing *Vacaloca*. Countless coins hail down.

Scene 3: *The collective suicide*

The Rock Musician pours drops of poison into the actors' mouths and they all scream and collapse to the ground. Silence descends. All of a sudden, I see the Chechnyan Refugee putting the first card into the Widow's mouth, a second near the Rock Musician's foot, and a third on the Rumanian Housewife's left shoulder, as in a funeral ceremony. The actors are awakened from their leaden sleep by the sound of the violin. The blindfolded Italian Violinist slowly brings them back to life with his music. The Young Colombian knocks three times on the floor. No answer. He keeps on desperately knocking and the sounds become louder and louder. Again, no answer. Absolute silence.

Scene 4: *Everybody knows*

The Mercenary pushes a wheelchair in this space that seems to be "a raft, the terrace of a building, a country, or even Europe" (Ledger 2012: 127). The Danish Lawyer takes a seat in the wheelchair and starts to sing the song *Everybody knows that the dice are loaded,* during which simultaneous actions are performed in a dynamic rhythm: the Rumanian Housewife cleans and cleans the floor; the Black Madonna handles the sword vigorously; the Rock Musician walks through the space with light steps; the Chechnyan Refugee spins around a man's suit preserved in a transparent bag that *evokes the past* (Varley 2011b: 43). Suddenly, I notice: the conflict between the Black Madonna and the Young Colombian; the Rumanian Housewife's toiling hands; the scenic objects which seem to wake up to life and dance – the movements of the cards touching the eyes, of the red handkerchief embracing the face; the rain of thousands and thousands of coins reminding us of the final scene from *My Father's House* in which the actors throw coins: "a shower of hail? stones? or 'just' money" (Nagel Rasmussen 2018: 99). It is a world in which suicide seems to be the only salvation. One needs nothing more than a cloth to cover eyes and nostrils and mouth. *Everybody knows that at the beginning there is always a wound* (Barba 1993b).

Scene 5: *The passport*

A game of 'who deceives who?' or the 'deceived thinks he deceives the deceiver'; waves and waves of coins are thrown during the sequence; a visa in one's passport costs money.

Scene 6: *The revolt*

The revolt of the Rock Musician who, whipping himself, howls: *God made me in fists, blood and bones! / A miserable rag wounded by the Lord's chisel / which penetrated flesh and blood. / He created me for ever greater pain. / You, sleeping friend, in front of me, / were more fortunate than me,* and lots of coins like bullets hunt him down piercing his bowed head and bent body. He raises his sad eyes to the sky, but instead of a blue sky he sees a blood red sky, and then he knows that there is no escape for anyone in this upside down world.

Scene 7: *My sister*

Scene 8: *Benedictus Domine*

"There is a country
made up of all the countries in the world,
and in this country there is a city
made up of all the cities in the country,
and in this city there is a street
made up of all the streets in the city,
and in this street there is a house
made up of all the houses in the street,
and in this house there is a room
and in this room there is a man
and this man is laughing,
laughing,
and no one has laughed like
He."
(Barba 1985b: 19)

Scene 9: *The parade of the sick souls*

Scene 10: *The tango of loneliness*

Or the dance of the lonely pairs, their gaze lost to the horizon. The Rumanian Housewife puts a mask on her face and ties the Young Colombian's neck to a leash. Are they preparing to go out for a walk? Is it an attempt to *domesticate* the young boy? Is there room only for domesticated animals in this Wonderland?

Scene 11: *Travelling a stretch of water*

'Shut the door!', shouts the Rumanian Housewife and soon after the Danish Lawyer lifts the door up, up, up, above his head, spins it around, and then places it on the table. Someone waves the Danish flag, and they all board a ship sailing to far away shores. Do they travel to new lands to leave their past behind? Heartbeats are heard. The *ship of stone* is pushed by the waves and the wind. And, here, in the middle of the waters, a crime is committed: the Rock Musician strangles the Young Colombian who is covered in the cloth of the flag. But the Black Madonna performs a miracle and saves him. However, he is brought to life only to commit, in turn, another murder: he shoots the Puppet. The traces of murder are wiped out by the Rumanian Housewife. The Mercenaries wrap the Puppet in the flag, bring a rusty metal barrel in which they throw the instruments, the angel wings and the flowers and then brutally roll the barrel out in the dazzling hail of coins. The Danish Lawyer offers a coin to the Young Colombian – the price he has to pay for his journey to the world of the dead? – who angrily screams: 'No, you are not my father!'

Scene 12: *The calvary*

'Saben morir solo con la bocca llena / To know how to die only with the mouth full': the Young Colombian raises the wooden door carved in deep narrow ditches from where rivulets of coins flow. On his way to Golgotha, he carries the door like a cross on his shoulders and begins singing. The door is metamorphosed into a bridge to an apparently strange unknown world where his steps carry him to the coffin where the Black Madonna waits for him. After she caresses him gently, they embrace, breathing the frozen air of death. At the end of their sequence, the mercenaries place the door on the coffin and engross themselves in playing a game of cards for money. 'Bingo!' exclaims the Danish Lawyer.

Scene 13: *The vicious circle*

The Violinist knocks three times on the floor, sits down at the table to be fed with plenty of coins. And he swallows full spoons with metal.

Fiskedam, 'fish hatchery', was called the actors' training during the period of creation of the performances Brecht's Ashes *and* The Million; *here each actor's little ideas found the ideal environment for their growth and Eugenio Barba could fish those that served him* (Carreri 2007: 111). Do the instruments, the wings, the flowers, the Puppet, the soldier's cap, the block of ice, the actors hanging from hooks like large pieces of meat, speak about the idea of the human being's vulnerable and ephemeral life?

Now the performance has a circular structure. It makes me think of the Ouroboros, of the eternal *cycle of life, death and rebirth*.

Wednesday, 6 October 2010, Holstebro

What is your father's face like?

Eugenio Barba: "I dare to trust the part of myself that I call the blind horse."
(Nagel Rasmussen 2018: 45)

Eugenio Barba works with Roberta Carreri and Jan Ferslev on their score which I entitled *the day-by-day happiness*. It is the happiness that lovers feel when they enjoy and share every word, every little thing, every action; when at home, love, minute by minute, floats in the air and your lover is always by your side, teasing, caressing, and embracing you tenderly.

The actors introduce in their score the song *Stand By Your Man*, which tells the story of a safe and stable bond. At the same time, their scene unveils the fact that the passions of gods or the burning love of Shakespearian characters can be felt also by ordinary people, nameless men and women, humble humans whose love, hate, dreams, sufferings, ideals and failures are kept under wraps.

Tage Larsen starts improvising with a book. What book is it? The Book of Life? The Bible? Julia Varley murmurs a gentle lullaby. Kai Bredholt moves quickly through the room with a bell on the top of his head. At a certain moment he starts running, carrying a tray full of glasses; unexpectedly he stumbles and drops it. I startle when I hear the deafening noise of the broken glass; suddenly all freezes: the air freezes, the actors and the participants freeze, except the director who, in perfect silence, picks up the pieces. A few seconds later, the actors resume their training.

I am fully engrossed in the rehearsal, attempting to notice each actor's minuscule impulse, the *real action* Eugenio Barba speaks about in *On Directing and Dramaturgy: Burning the House,* chapter *Real actions, improvisation and score*: "When in the training or during rehearsals I divided any situation (like writing a letter and putting it into an envelope, peeling an apple or picking up a coin from the ground) into smaller and smaller segments, I reached an indivisible point, a barely perceptible atom: a minute dynamic form which nevertheless had consequences for the tone of the whole body. This minute dynamic form was called *a real action* by me and my actors. It could be microscopic, just an impulse, however it radiated within the whole organism and was immediately sensed by the nervous system of the spectator" (Barba 2010a: 26). So, Roberta Carreri takes me by surprise when she whispers in my ear: 'Eugenio has asked me to speak my lines in Romanian'. All of a sudden, I feel happy. Such a beautiful, gorgeous, unexpected present! I am speechless, incapable of expressing my feelings of joy and gratitude. 'Would you like to translate the text?', she asks me, still whispering. 'Yes ... right ... certainly ... gladly ... happily ...', I answer, feeling an overwhelming happiness.

The same day, Roberta gives me the text in Italian:

Tutto cominciò su una nave
arenata nel deserto

Torgeir!
Non ci hai mai offerto niente
di così leggero

Che faccia ha tuo padre
Tutti i padri sono veri
Allora è nel lago
è piuttosto lui che dovrebbero pescare
i pesci ne hanno lasciato solo le ossa
Costa denaro

Ti canteranno la storia
E col passare del tempo
Ti benderanno gli occhi
Come hanno fatto a me
Ti mostreranno l'ascia
E passato un pò di tempo
Ti nasconderanno l'albero
Come hanno fatto a me
Non ti servirà a nulla
Sapere la verità
Se quando gridi nessuno ascolterà

Adesso basta!
Lo stiamo ricordando

Non c'è nessuna pietà qui,
nessuna misericordia

Welcome! Benvenuta!

Figlia di puttana

Avevo diciassette anni quando vidi
Per la prima volta il mare

We begin to work. Roberta Carreri helps me, explaining to me the subtle nuances within the text. I never dreamed of a day when Roberta and I would work together. She has interpreted her lines in Romanian magnificently!

Thursday, 7 October 2010, Holstebro

Omar Khayyám

8 pm: *Omar Khayyám – Poesi på en torsdag / Poetry on a Thursday*. The guest poets tonight are Jens Blendstrup and Lars Bukdahl. Amphitryon: Ulrik Skeel.

A few days before. It is lunch break. I hurry to the kitchen. I crave a cup of hot coffee. I meet Ulrik Skeel. 'Diana, tell me, do you know if Omar Khayyám's poems are translated into Romanian?', he asks me. Omar Khayyám, Omar Khayyám, I repeat his name in my head. And I vaguely remember one year I was given a bilingual Romanian-French edition for my birthday. 'Perhaps. I am not sure. I will search on the Internet', I say in a low murmur, answering his question. 'Would you like to recite some of his quatrains, in the Romanian language, on our next Thursday poetry reading?' 'Yes, gladly!' I cry happily and run to my room to start a Google search. I am excited to discover a few quatrains translated into Romanian. I read and re-read them, write them on sheets of paper, rehearse the verses many a time. In the evening, plunged in a sweet reverie, I let myself be carried away by the beauty and musicality of the verses about love and loss, yearning to live my life to the fullest. Near midnight, I go to sleep still rehearsing the Rubáiyát dear to me:

LIV
But if in vain, down on the stubborn floor
Of Earth, and up to Heav'n's unopening Door,
You gaze TO-day, while You are You—how then
TO-morrow, You when shall be You no more?

LXVI
Oh threats of Hell and Hopes of Paradise
One thing at least is certain—This Life flies;
One thing is certain and the rest is Lies;
The Flower that once is blown for ever dies.

LXXIII
We are no other than a moving row
Of visionary Shapes that come and go
Round with this Sun-illumin'd Lantern held
In Midnight by the Master of the Show

LXVII
Strange, is it not? that of the myriads who
Before us pass'd the door of Darkness through
Not one returns to tell us of the Road,
Which to discover we must travel too.
(Khayyám 1909)

Friday, 8 October 2010, Holstebro

Ancora una volta – Once again

Eugenio Barba works patiently on the micro-scenes. Paying careful attention to every action, every sound, every step, every relationship, he often tells the actors: *ancora una volta*.

His detailed work with Kai Bredholt on his vocal and physical actions is part of the creative process in which the actor focuses on the organicity of execution. About his struggle with routine, Bredholt remarks: "I invented small 'mistakes' that could help me: an action a little bit delayed or anticipated, a small counter impulse, or just a thought like I want to go to the right, but I go to the left. These small 'mistakes' became conscious musical accents, until each action had its own identity" (Bredholt 2011: 32). I cannot take my eyes off the way they work on the precision and rigour of the actions.

The first scene of the performance-work in progress *portrays a state of mind*: in a sober atmosphere imbued with sadness, the spectator is invited to take part in a ritual of death. The space which appears to be coloured in red and black enhances the spectator's senses so that he feels the devastation of losing a loved one. The scene has the power of a spell. I am totally attracted into this magical moment in which the spoken words and actions seem to be part of the *language of life*. It is a scene about the ephemeral life and eternal death, about struggle and emptiness, about a boy who gives all of himself to save his father and fails. And even though the spectator perceives only the tip of the iceberg, looking beyond the characters' surface behaviour he feels deep down inside the despair and sorrow rooted in their actions.

The second scene, swarming with human beings who survived the war, is built through simultaneous actions. Silence and stillness alternate with singing and dynamic movements. A nightmarish story about restrained desires, uprooting, loss, mutilation, flagellation, a story that tells us that it is essential for one to stay alive even when one has lost any reason to live.

'Ancora una volta!'

Monday, 11 October 2010, Holstebro

Hell is murky (Shakespeare 2005: 142)

"Out, damned spot", Queen Macbeth's maddening words seem to come out of the Rumanian Housewife's mouth who wipes and wipes stains only she can see. Limping and moaning, at times, her behaviour resembles that of an abandoned animal, seeking for shelter and kindness, crying under the heavy burden of loneliness; a sick being who, longing to fly, tiptoes and raises her wings but, alas, only for one second, for instantly her body bends and falls to the ground. An angel falls. An angel whose turquoise wings are no more than humble crutches. She dreams she can fly, and she cannot; actually she is *condemned to swallow, masticate and vomit*, to join the endless queue of the *victims of duty* waiting to die. Perhaps she feels an unstoppable desire to bury herself alive in her dear memories or perhaps her dear memories make her unable to breathe. That is why she puts a plastic bag over her head, ties it tightly around her neck, and tries to suffocate herself. In vain. She fails. "Out, I say! – One, two – why, then 'tis time to do't" (Shakespeare 2005: 142), Lady Macbeth's line springs to mind. Murder and suicide. To kill a man and to kill yourself. The Rumanian Housewife tries again. She fails again and tries again. But she cannot kill herself. She cannot escape her nightmare like Lady Macbeth who cannot escape the smell of her murder: "Here's the smell of the blood, still. All the perfumes of Arabia will not sweeten this little hand" (Shakespeare 2005: 143). And then the Rumanian Housewife puts a mask on her face. What for? To hide her true feelings and thoughts from herself, from others? Vainly. The mask sickens her soul. The mask does not help her escape the swarm of her suicidal thoughts. It is the mask behind which she is dead, whilst still living.

Who knows what he reads in his little book

Everybody knows that the boat is leaking…, and yet what do we do in the meantime? Seek the truth of existence in the Book of Life? Open it, breathe life into it, turn the pages, wander through its fictional world. Reading avidly, we devour the fruits of knowledge; in fact, we search, consciously-unconsciously, for *the word that we lost;* it is the key word capable of filling our life with a sense; for some, this word is love, for others, is truth; we look for it in precious books or in exciting experiences.

The Danish Lawyer opens a little book and, holding it delicately with his fingers, he begins to read. Who knows what he reads in his book? Driven by a strong desire to discover secrets from his past, perhaps he finds out why he loves white roses or why he feels the impulse to throw himself into the fight with the Angel. Yes. Perhaps. Who knows what he learns from his little book. He closes it and leaves the space with a thoughtful air.

Soon he reappears to practise different postures. And now he is cheerful with his body bending backwards, and a second later he is sad with his hands shoved in the pockets of his trousers. He no longer has in his hands a book, but a passport and begins performing one of his magic tricks, the passport trick: 'Look at the passport! Here it is! Here it is not! Where is it? Hehehe! One, two, three! Here it is! Oh, no, it is not!'. I am, at once, caught up in his little world of illusions.

The Chechnyan Refugee performs her actions with the aim of persuading the Danish Lawyer to facilitate her entry in the Wonderland. To achieve her goal, she tries to trick him, playing the role of a helpless woman. So she gets down on her knees, begging him to help her. Apparently impressed by her sheeplike attitude, the Danish Lawyer raises her up, takes her by the shoulders, warms her in his coat, but suddenly becomes angry and pushes her. She could not have him in! He has tricked her by playing the role of a good, open-hearted guy. A role, no more than that. A sly smile broadens on his face while he lays the passport on the ground and pushes her towards it. With faltering steps, trembling in fear, she nears the passport. She snatches it and the Danish Lawyer stamps it with a small stone. There are a few moments of euphoria. But suddenly he throws the stone violently so that, upon hitting the floor, it makes a lugubrious sound; and then he pushes her again and again. She falls down severely hurting herself. There is a price for any gain. He bursts into laughter and makes his exit.

Wednesday, 13 October 2010, Holstebro

Skeletons with red flowers between their teeth

The beginning of the performance unveils the image of a dark dawn rising in icy silence, in soberness, in man's acceptance of the plate of irony that life serves him up when it displays the Card of Death. The Widow of a Basque Officer assuages our ancestral fears telling us: "Just take it as it is!"

From dark dawn to blue dawn: the sky-blue of the wings, of the silky, soft, snake-like shawl tied around Lolito's neck, of the Danish Lawyer's fine leather suit, of the rusty iron the trash barrel is made of; the blue-sky of the eyes; the purple-blue of the kiss of death.

It seems that the Rumanian Housewife keeps watch over the house. Is she the owner of the keys that open certain doors? Which doors? I wonder. The door to Inferno? To Paradise? Does man go to Paradise when he dies? Or to Inferno? Nobody knows. Some say that Paradise and Inferno exist inside us. It is true. There are times when we feel the joy of Paradise, and times when we feel the fire of Inferno. It all depends on how we live our lives. Still. What kind of life? *A chronic life?*

Does the Rumanian Housewife have her own door? Is it open? Shut? Is there a new life awaiting her outside this house of despair? She wants to break free from her chronic nightmares, from the images of war crimes, from life's injustice. She wants. But she is helpless. Perhaps, for her, it is all for nothing. Or, perhaps she has to wait for the moment she will sing her swan song. In this respect, Roberta Carreri tells us: "I sing a new song while I use the turquoise wings: *What a Wonderful World*. I sing it blindfolded before the second suicide attempt" (Carreri 2011: 67). Desire to put an end to life. To her chronic life.

Then what good is it to have two keys hanging around her neck as a talisman? What good is it to look after a house wherein her life has been torn to pieces? How can she still have a ray of hope inside this sick house? A house destroyed by war. What good is it, for her, to cry out: "Shut the door!"? What good is it? *To be well out of the draught?* (Pinter 1971: 11) Perhaps. Nevertheless, it seems that she has not lost her hope of living a happy life. Perhaps in this house there is a secret door. Hidden in the wall. Or perhaps there are many secret doors. A door *for each of them*. On this point, Ferdinando Taviani remarks: *There is a dead who is not dead, a boy who stirs out of the coffin he was put in, or who turned himself in to seek his peace. He comes out, ceases to seek and suffer – finally, he smiles. There is a blind twin next to him. The latter plays the violin in such a way that we can only feel excited after having been moved by the fanfare and the songs full of vitality. Excited – each of us in his own way. The long-imprisoned and isolated twins now find open doors. They laugh like children who go out of the house to play. They leave in frozen silence* (Barba 2012a: IX). Where do they go? In search for their personal path lit by a twinkling star?

Some, overfed, eat without being hungry and drink without being thirsty. Stuffed with goodies, for them, caviar tastes like sand.

Others, victims of war, eat without being hungry and drink without being thirsty as life, for them, lost its taste and fragrance, for it lost its sense. In an upside down world, those who succeeded in escaping the sickle of war look for shelter to heal their wounds. But there are wounds that can never be healed: dreams and ideals, families and friends crushed under the brutal boots of the soldiers in a never-ending world war. Filippo Tommaso Marinetti's sarcastic shouts come to my mind: "Yes, war! Against all of you who are dying too slowly, and against all the dead who are clogging the streets!" as "To their vacillating lives, broken by dismal agonies, by fearful dreams and burdensome nightmares, we prefer a violent death and we exalt it as the only one worthy of man, that beast of prey" (Marinetti 2009a: 54). Lacking the Marinettian delusion of grandeur, the characters, in *The Chronic Life*, seem to be *the dead who clog the streets* after the war is over! Ill beings with their minds, bodies and souls for ever mutilated. For them, the war is not the only *hygiene of the world*, but the worst experience of their lives. *All war is a symptom of man's failure as a thinking animal* (John Steinbeck). Failure. Céline tells us. Eugène Ionesco tells us. At the end of *Rhinoceros*, only one man, an ordinary man, Bérenger, remains.

In a senseless world there is no *daily heroism*. No heroic destinies. No heroes. Only skeletons with red flowers between their teeth.

Friday, 15 October 2010, Holstebro

Sad sick snail

The atmosphere is incandescent when the rehearsal reaches its peak form! Preparations for Wrocław where open rehearsals will be held for worldwide participants in the *Masters in Residence* programme.

I ask myself again and again: Does the chronic life produce a slow degradation of man's spirit? Does it sap his courage in his fight for freedom? Is man ridiculed for his ideas and ideals? Do we witness the final battle between spiritual and carnal forces? Between good and evil?

Man has transformed himself into a monster who waves the flag of war, of endless wars, till there will be no war for there will be none to wave the flag. No more living world.

Chronic illness: hatred and self-devouring hatred; envy, covetousness and greed; selfishness and coldness; cruelty; manipulative strategies; lack of scruples; ruthlessness; lies, deception and controlled anger to force one's victim into submission; human sacrifice; fear.

Chronic life: suicide attempt, lie, illusion, nightmare, no way out.

No matter which road one takes, death always waits for him at the end of the road. In the lonely hour, man realises that the rehearsal for death has been preparing him for dying. Still, he believes that if he had drunk from the golden cup full of the elixir of life, he would probably have lived for ever.

To live without love is to die slowly in a cold bed inside a cold dungeon.

A story about suffocation.

Characters from different countries seek shelter in a plundered world reduced to the shell of a sad, sick snail.

Tuesday, 20 October 2010, Wrocław

Working on something invisible: energy
(Barba-D'Urso 2000: 64)

At nine sharp, the training begins at Studio Na Grobli. The huge hall is crammed with participants. The space glows in the light of the sun rays which invade in through the large glasses of the windows, inducing the strange sensation that you are in the hall of the lost steps.

The actors are engrossed in the execution of their sequences of actions. Eugenio Barba's interventions are quick, prompt, energetic. All participants are fascinated by the demonstration of their work.

Wednesday, 21 October 2010, Wrocław

At home

Is the *observer* a privileged spectator who he has been offered the possibility of witnessing the artists' work-in-progress? Undoubtedly, the answer is *yes*. I have learnt about Odin Teatret's *tradition-in-life* from Eugenio Barba's books and articles. But the real lesson to be learned from his dramaturgy takes place in the rehearsal space. Empathising with the director, I am lost in admiration for his creative vision. At the same time, I wonder if some of the observers' reactions are similar or close to the reactions of his *spectators-fetishes*.

An observer is *a person who observes an important event so that he can tell other people about it*. But one's perceptions are limited. Not to say that many times not only one's view of himself affects his perceptions but also his prejudices and daily routine have an influence on his ways of perceiving and understanding an event, a situation, a person's behaviour or a scene. Due to his limited perceptions, the observer is not capable of perceiving, for instance, an entire scene. Grasping a small part of it, he instantaneously fills in the gaps, using his imagination.

I feel *at home* in the rehearsal room taking great delight in decoding the 'drawings' made by the actors with their feet on the floor. Knowing that in Barba's dramaturgy the tiniest scenic action has multiple meanings, I realise I will never be capable of deciphering the enigma of the performance. There are so many stories hidden behind the actions.

Limits of perception. Limits of understanding. Limits.

The language of angels to which Eugenio Barba referred yesterday still preoccupies me.

Friday, 22 October 2010, Wrocław

A decisive no (!) to cock-a-doodle-doo!

How many stories does the face of an artist tell?

How closely is training linked to spirituality, refinement of the mind?

Is there a difference between a *domesticated* mind-body and a *tamed* mind-body?

Sometimes the individual's speech seems to be reduced to specialised words or verbal stereotypes, to *cock-a-doodle-doo!* or *oink-oink!* or *woof-woof!* or to: "There, it's nine o'clock. We've drunk the soup, and eaten the fish and chips, and the English salad. The children have drunk English water. We've eaten well this evening. [...] Potatoes are very good fried in fat; the salad oil was not rancid. The oil from the grocer at the corner is better quality than the oil from the grocer across the street. It is even better than the oil from the grocer at the bottom of the street" (Ionesco 1958: 9).

A performance, like a book or a painting, is an *opera aperta*. The spectator enters the fictional reality of the performance willing to *read* the director's vision with which he may empathise or not, that he may share or not, or in which he may recognise himself or not. In order to do so, the spectator has to detach himself from himself and prepare for the moment he sets out on his journey through the fictitious universe. Only if the spectator forgets himself in this imagined world, only if he truly *listens to* the director's story, will he experience a change.

I think it is essential to overcome our conditioned reflexes, prejudices, stereotypes in behaviour, daily *cock-a-doodle-doo*. And I think this is what *The Chronic Life* reminds us.

Saturday, 23 October 2010, Wrocław

Link in the chain

I love rehearsals. They are so vulnerable. And so rarely does someone have the courage to reveal the *vulnerability* Eugenio Barba speaks about when referring to *My Father's House*: "I sensed a vulnerability in myself which I also found in the actors, and which I have since considered to be one of the most important qualities in our work: the ability or courage to reveal one's vulnerability" (Nagel Rasmussen 2018: 93).

Every day, I note down my thoughts and the sensations experienced during rehearsals. While imagining possible future actions and relationships, I am tempted to revisit the already existing scenes, to meditate upon their clusters of meanings, to find possible links between them.

A possible link in the chain:

The Black Madonna seems to be a deity descended among the spectators. Limping, she carries in a soldier's helmet, hangs it from a hook, embraces the Puppet and prays over him; then she nears the end wall and crouches till she becomes one with the red bricks. The Widow, half man half woman, an androgynous figure, limping, enters carrying a plate, cutlery and napkins; she feeds the Puppet as a mother feeds her sick little child, watches over him as she knows that death will menace him in the near future. The Young Colombian comes in; he and the Puppet are dressed identically as both of them will share the same destiny; the Widow teaches him how to wash the dying man, to say goodbye to him. And then the young boy starts to walk, and he walks as if he is in a deep sleep; he walks, and his walk becomes a run with the block of ice in his arms. A run in a deadly circle for there is no escape, no place to go to, no dream to be dreamed, for death is already present. A run during which a room becomes a street and the street becomes a house and the house becomes another room in which a man is dying; and in his maddening run to arrive in time to save a life, he is surrounded by invisible walls; the invisible walls incessantly wiped by the Rumanian Housewife with repetitive gestures. Holding on to his block of ice, the boy falls to the ground; and it is then that he feels tired and useless. The Widow puts the piece of ice under the dying Puppet's head and prays.

When the Black Madonna exits with the Puppet in her arms, the Chechnyan Refugee, "dressed as a woman, a refugee from the Caucasus or the Near East" (Varley 2011b: 48) bursts into the space. "Exile, deportation, refugee" are keywords that describe her character: "the widow of a man who went to war, perhaps as a soldier, perhaps as a guerrilla fighter, and who has not returned; perhaps he was killed, perhaps he disappeared" (Varley 2011b: 48). The scene in which the Chechnyan Refugee places her pan and green metal chest in the storeroom and then presents her merchandise, bright-coloured tablecloths, to the spectators, is a scene about uprooting and rooting in foreign soil.

The Rumanian Housewife limps in grotesquely, hangs her blue wings on hooks and then starts decorating the table. The Danish Lawyer places a seven-branched menorah with lit candles on the table. The Rock Musician plays the electric guitar, the Chechnyan Refugee attempts to trick the Danish Lawyer into getting her passport while the Rumanian Housewife seems to be haunted by dark memories. Heaps and heaps of coins fall to the ground. The actors dance in circle till they get tired and crouch down. In an ecstatic state, the Black Madonna with the Puppet in her arms, traverses the stage. Now the war is symbolised by the candle flame. In a gloomy scenic space, the moment the Puppet's fingers touch the flame, the Puppet dies: another child, innocent victim, cradled in the lethal rhythm of war. Then the Rock Musician makes a ghastly apparition into this morbid space that resembles a burial chamber. I feel myself being immersed in the macabre atmosphere of Edgar Allan Poe's short stories. Suddenly he begins to whip the coffin with such violence as if he wants to beat death and a second later he whips himself as if he wants to put an end to his miserable life. The scene reaches its climax when the Rumanian Housewife and the Chechnyan Refugee dance frantically. Silence descends on the stage. Total stillness. It is a moment of peace that I feel deep inside me. However, it does not last long. There is war again. "Shut the door! Shut the door! Shut the door!", the Rumanian Housewife cries passionately.

Welding flames flicker somewhere up behind the black curtain. All actors, singing *La vacaloca*, carry the musical instruments and the blue wings to the cemetery. Someone beats a nail into the bleeding heart of Madonna-Kali who sticks out her tongue for a few seconds. Apparently all hope is lost forever. Madonna-Kali, an immortal deity, is transformed into a mortal creature.

Why, sometimes, *someone or something turns out to be nobody or nothing*?

And, then, where to go in this world void of love, of hope?

Have you found out what you have been looking for?

It is October 2010. Tage Larsen and I eat our lunch at Studio Na Grobli. "Have you found out what you have been looking for?", he asks me with a smile. "No", I answer him and go on, "I have just felt a terrible desire to think out loud! I have not uttered a single word in a whole month!". He laughs warmly and nods as if he knows exactly what is hidden behind my words. Yes. Perhaps he knows.

I almost run to the terrace as I feel like smoking a cigarette after our conversation. Yes, I think, even after long years of experience, Tage Larsen, an intelligent and cultivated actor, has not lost his vitality and gargantuan appetite for theatre. It is evident that not only his remarkable acting, striking presence, exceptional voice, but also his versatility, creative thinking, and great sense of humour have ensured him enduring fame. Subtly estranged from himself and from his character, the Danish Lawyer, the actor reveals *his enormous emotional force coupled with a certain cool distance, a disconcerting irony* (Nagel Rasmussen 2018: 93). His powerful artistic personality, charming and expressive presence, commitment to mental-physical-vocal training, vivid imagination, capacity to dig deep into himself and into his characters' inner lives, make him a great actor.

I really miss the ironic twinkle in his blue eyes.

Monday, 25 October 2010, Wrocław

Tempus fugit

Today Eugenio Barba changes *the space-horseshoe* with *the space-river*. The scenic space seems familiar to me.

I intend to revisit the sequence of *Jacob's wrestling with the Angel* and to investigate in-depth *the cosmogonical myths* (see Eugenio Barba and Mircea Eliade).

Tuesday, 1 February 2011, Holstebro

Hope still resides inside our hearts

"I would like *The Chronic Life* to open a tiny crack into the dark incandescent magma of the individual and his painstaking vital zigzagging to free himself from an icy embrace: that of the implacable and indifferent Great Mother of Abortions and Shipwrecks, Our Lady History." (Barba 2011a: 8)

The Chronic Life reminds me of the people who, living in the former communist countries of Eastern Europe, totally deprived of freedom, sought refuge in their dreams with eyes open. Their lives were split between two powerful tendencies: inaction and action, that is dream and fight for their dream of freedom to become real; many of them fought for it with a force and passion similar to those of the Greek tragic heroes.

Barba's performance, *a blasphemy against our beliefs* (Monsalve 2011: 24), *dedicated to Anna Politkovskaya and Natalia Estemirova, Russian writers and human right activists, murdered by anonymous thugs in 2006 and 2009 for their opposition to the Chechen conflict*, tells the story of a young boy, a little bit older than a child, who does not integrate into society and has the courage to leave it behind. The story takes place in 2031. Speaking about human suffering, uprooting, despair, loneliness, loss of faith, the director presents us with the future of *a world turned upside down* in which characters bent beneath the weight of their burden look for shelter. The war with oneself and with the other is the dominant theme of the performance. We must not forget that both individuals and societies have been in a permanent state of war, that "Wars were wrapped in religious cloaks. The internal wars among the intransigent Christian factions reproduced in Europe the clash between Christianity, Islam and paganism all over the planet. Within the single individual, equivalent struggles opposed the hope of Salvation to the terror of Damnation" (Barba 2006: 2). In this devastated world, while the sound of Günter Grass' *tin drum* reverberates painfully, paradoxically, the characters have not lost totally their hunger for life. They still dream of love, beauty, harmony, truth and happiness. They still have hope. It is the apocalyptic-regenerating end of the performance that reminds me that hope still resides inside our hearts.

In the Odin Teatret library, Eugenio Barba speaks enthusiastically about possible *points of contact* between the actors' actions, about *simultaneities*; the director renounces the idea of having "a crystal coffin full of water in which an eel and a drowned girl swim" (Barba 2011b: 9), but does not give up the idea of water: "'Let the rain come', the director exclaimed, 'in affluence'" (Nagel Rasmussen 2011: 72). Another flood?

A return to the *primordial soup*? Or a possible rebirth of mother-nature? A second life as *the time for spring, for virgin energies is within us* "at the end of a war, amid mourning and devastation. Incomprehensibility which is tinged with hope". *There is hope in the end of the performance for* "The actors move away from pain and desperation shaken by an invisible yet audible thread: music" (Barba 2011b: 9).

The first day of rehearsals is full of excitement.

The Puppet, dressed neatly in a white shirt, greenish trousers and brown boots, looks innocent, pure and cute in the gloomy and depressing freshly painted scenic space veiled in sadness.

Changes in the scenic space: the platform and the wooden wall painted grey, shades of milky grey, make me think of a strange realm of existence. The red-orange metal hooks look like weird animals lurking in the darkness, waiting to attack. The table-bed-coffin covered in a white sheet fills the centre space. There are times when the wooden door suggests the image of a dragon with multiple heads preventing foreigners from entering the promised land. A black curtain hangs at the opposite end of the scenic space. The red curtain that obstructs the spectator's view of the space reminds me of *The Gospel according to Oxyrhincus* in which: "A curtain divided the two banks of spectators preventing them from noticing their mutual presence. Behind the curtain, the spectators imagined the performing space with the actors. Suddenly the curtain fell, and the spectators believed they were seeing their own reflection in a mirror" (Barba 2010a: 47).

I wonder: does the characters' deep existential crises make the spectator taste the bitterness of his incompleteness, loss and failure? Yes. Failure could be a keyword. *The one who fails is the one who acts according to a programme he no longer believes in* (Culianu 2010: 124). Or the one who fails is the one who loses the courage to change what he wants to be changed, the courage to wake up to a *new* day every day, the courage to fight for his ideas and ideals. Yes. It is so easy to fail. And then it is as if one feels his mind rotted, his vital forces disintegrated, his mouth full of sand, or it is as if one transforms himself into a *rhinoceros* (Ionesco). Yes. Perhaps it is all about failure.

Now rehearsals are held in the Red room.

Wednesday, 2 February 2011, Holstebro

The performance is written on stage

As I watch the rehearsals from the upper row of seats, from time to time, I have the sensation of dizziness, feeling as if I am going to fall. The images of the Wonderland resemble those of a world on fire that drags me into its womb; these are the moments in rehearsals when I feel as if I am riding a *merry-go-round*.

Everything is on the move. The actors enrich their scores with new texts. The director establishes the relationships between characters, introduces a song in the Black Madonna's score, changes one of her exits with the Puppet, explores the nature of the relationship between the Chechnyan Refugee and the spectators.

When the sound of trumpets fills the air, the Black Madonna starts running with the Puppet in her arms. She stops in front of the lit candles and stares at the dancing flames. *Glowing with fervour and rebellion*, she dryly concludes: "We are a planet without children". The Puppet's little fingers slowly touch the flames. Fire. Fire. Fire. Death. There is such a difference between the fire of war and *the fire of the acting*: "Theatre is the 'land of fire'. When speaking of performance, especially among professionals and connoisseurs, the idea of fire returns as a leitmotiv: the *fire* of the acting, the audience that is *inflamed*, the *ardour* of passions and applause. When a comedy is *brilliant* and *sparks,* when the tragic actor *glows* with fervour and rebellion or the actress *blazes* with scorn or a desire for revenge, the spectators, petrified yet happy, are touched by doubt: is it just their impression or is a fire brooding somewhere?" (Barba 2008: 1)

Barba adds a new text to the Rumanian Housewife's score: "Am două chei: una pentru uşa ţării pe care o caut şi una pentru uşa ţării pe care am pierdut-o. O cheie pentru uşa mamei mele şi una pentru uşa fiicei mele / I have two keys: one for the door to the country I search for and one for the door to the country I lost. A key for the door of my mother and a key for the door of my daughter".

Thursday, 3 February 2011, Holstebro

A new scene

The flames of the candles intensifying the feeling of sorrow one may feel when surrounded by the shadows of loneliness produce "an atmosphere alive with sudden and volatile shadows, far removed from the docility of our domesticated electricity" (Barba 2008: 1), evoking the idea that: "we must not forget that theatre is fiction in transit toward another reality, toward the refusal of the reality that we presume to know. Theatre is fiction that can change both those people who act as well as those who observe" (Barba 2008: 3). So it happens that while listening to the actors' singing, I immerse into their ocean of music where I stay still, afraid I might disturb their rehearsal.

A new scene of strong eroticism between the Rock Musician and the Young Colombian, conceived as an androgynous figure, is created. The Rock Musician touches tenderly the boy's body with his feet, caressing lustfully the erogenous zones; then, suddenly, he grabs the body and takes it into his possession while in the meantime the Rumanian Housewife moans, haunted by her nightmares. Terrifying sounds of sexual pleasure and pain fill in the space.

Sometimes the strange sounds and silences seem to be visited by the shadows of forgotten or concealed stories of love, light and ecstasy.

Friday, 4 February 2011, Holstebro

Domesticated light

Every morning, the actors rehearse their songs. Today Jan Ferslev conducts the music rehearsal. As I listen to their singing, sequences from *Inside the Skeleton of the Whale* come to my mind. At the same time, the actors' vocal modulations make me think that *there is a plurality of worlds, the actor is not a definitive form, but a form which can be filled with varied sonorous contents* (Culianu 2010: 99).

The actors are singers, dancers and creators of their *organic dramaturgy*. Sometimes the force of their sounds is so much alike to the force of Sa'id ibn Misjah's sound who "discovered the properties of the sound when he was in great danger of being killed by a thief who, raising his sword, was at the point of splitting his skull. Sa'id ibn Misjah was so afraid that he uttered an inaudible cry which made the thief bend and succumb" (Culianu 1992: 28). It is the inner force capable "of designing phonic models in this world, filling them with compact substance, making them tangible, colourful, briefly – sensitive" (Culianu 1992: 32); it is the force of the actor who, through his body-voice, creates worlds undreamed by the spectator.

With an enigmatic smile, Eugenio Barba asks Fausto Pro for a "warm blue" and the latter, stupefied, mutters: "Warm blue does not exist". They look at each other for a few seconds and start laughing. Yes. There is warm blue *in the heaven above us and in the heaven inside us*. Not in the *domesticated light*.

Monday, 7 February 2011, Holstebro

The moment of the angel

It seems that the child's path of maturation at some point splits: on the one hand, maturation implies a sort of killing one's innocence, natural tendency to see the world in amazement, as one is supposed to become a pragmatic adult, a perfect small wheel in a perfect social system/machine; on the other hand, one never ceases hunting his ideals, yearning to fulfil his dreams, maintaining his curiosity for new knowledge and experiences. The latter represents the path of the artist, of the actor who endeavours to re-discover his deeper self during the training and work in the theatre laboratory: "All laboratories form actors that have not only physical abilities but also a 'different' mentality. A difference that has been given a variety of new names: ethics, spirituality, a love for art. But which is the necessary consequence of a body that is not only gymnastic and well-trained but also accustomed to reacting and speaking in its own disturbing language, ever changing, mysterious and unexpectedly profound, which some great theatres have shown us" (Schino 2009: 206). Sometimes it is as if the rehearsals for *The Chronic Life* take place in an alchemical laboratory where the nature of the spectator is examined under the microscope.

Eugenio Barba works with Roberta Carreri on the sequence which I have entitled *The moment of the angel*: spreading her huge blue wings, the actress nears the table, and slowly rising on tiptoe, climbs onto it; here she raises her wings but, losing her balance, her wings become crutches she heavily leans on; as in a trance she utters the words: "We dream", and returns to the *storeroom*.

The Rumanian Housewife buries her face in a napkin. The Chechnyan Refugee hides her face in the man suit. The Black Madonna covers her face with a red handkerchief. The Rock Musician, blindfolded with a strip of black leather, and the Danish Lawyer, his eyes covered with white artificial roses, apparently want to start a fight to the death. All of them try to hide their tears of sorrow inside their broken hearts. All of them refuse to see the reality of the world that surrounds them. All of them are trapped in a suffocating reality. A reality in which nothing ever changes. They have been spinning and spinning in a vicious circle, estranging themselves from themselves. A never-ending dance of regrets. A world in which all, brothers and sisters, suffer together and hope one day they will sing again: "Rise, Sister, winter is over, the flowers appear in the fields, the time for singing has returned" (Barba 1985b: 15).

During rehearsal, there are times when I react like the patient Thomas Bredsdorff refers to in his text *The Chronic Theatre*, that is *I react to seeing images, apparently devoid of meaning, by relating them to my own personal experiences* (Bredsdorff 2011:12). Perhaps that is why I think the performance should have a happy end. Perhaps that is why I long "to see a laughing child behind the mask of death" (Barba-Taviani 2004: 49). Perhaps that is why I hope that innocence can never be erased.

Tuesday, 8 February 2011, Holstebro

What is the secret of the whole originality? Work!

Eugenio Barba works with Iben Nagel Rasmussen: she runs, then climbs on the table, and runs again, then kicks the Rock Musician down, and runs again, then singing wildly she nears the Puppet and caresses him. Moving freely, she enters an ecstatic dance; at times, it is as if the unstoppable force of the ancestral Berserker emanates from her! Director and actress work in symbiosis! Director and actress are *one*. The sequence is relevant for their working process: "What is exceptional about Eugenio [Barba] is that he *allows things to grow*. He knows how to renounce ideas and accept the birth of something living, even if no one apparently desired it or searched for it, even if at the time he does not know what it can be used for, and even if it is quite different from what he had thought to be right and necessary. He knows how to react without hiding behind ideas. He changes" (Nagel Rasmussen 2018: 284).

It is today that the director gives Roberta Carreri a new text: *È piu facile far passare un cammello per la cruna di un ago che far passare uno straniero per la porta che tutela la nostra libertà / It is easier for a camel to pass through the eye of a needle than for a foreigner to step over the door which safeguards our freedom* (a paraphrase from the *New Testament*), and works on Iben Nagel Rasmussen's scene with the blind and crippled Puppet: 1. she walks through the space holding the Puppet like a baby or a trophy; 2. she carries him on her back like Christ carrying the cross; 3. she drags him along the floor; while she performs her sequence of actions, the actors dance in circle.

Speaking about the science of working with the impulse, Barba remarks: "What is the secret of the whole originality? Work!". And he works patiently on *the scene of the door.*

Wednesday, 9 February 2011, Holstebro

Sparkle-thoughts

"It is the fate of the seed to give birth to the fruit and remain hidden in it." (Ruffini 2010: 215)

"Credere nell'amore è la chiave / Io ho due chiavi / Una chiave per la porta di mia madre / E una chiave per la porta di mia figlia // To believe in love is the key / I have two keys / A key for the door of my mother / And a key for the door of my daughter // A crede în iubire este cheia / Am două chei / O cheie pentru uşa mamei mele / Şi o cheie pentru uşa fiicei mele", and we repeat many times, Roberta Carreri and I, the vowels 'ă' and 'î'.

Scenic presence with multiple faces.

"There is no limit to the perfection of an art." (Mei Lan Fang 1986: 32)

The lawyer has a small book with a black cover in one hand and a stone in the other hand, he places the stone on the ground, puts his foot on it and raises the small book, up-up, and the small book-larva metamorphoses into a butterfly.

Micro-action. Lightning-action. The look outside and the look inside, the look which strikes and the look which radiates vitality.

On "the effect of a 'different life' that a performance may generate in the spectator". (Schino 2009: 22)

Seventeen years? The love for theatre wakes you up early in the morning; when love dies, your daily life ritual is emptied, void of its vertical sense, the only sense worthy of letting yourself be wrapped in the warm fur of the movement.

Are you still human if you wait for the others to pull your strings?

Each with the reality of his consciousness. Each generous with himself.

Chekhov and his dialogue – parallel monologues: one sings lying in the bed-coffin, one marches, one throws confetti made out of cards, one cries: "Vivat Eugenio! Vivat Eugenio! Vivat OM! Vivat OM!".

"Everybody is happy" – "I skyggen vi vanke / blandt lysgrønne strå / In the shade we wander / among bright green straw". Yes. Everybody is happy.

It rains coins, in the rhythm of the heartbeat, so we will never forget that our chronic life is a parade of sick beings hand in hand with their children.

Run like you run for the last time, run like you'd be a storm and you'd rain and you'd wash all your wounds, run like you'd be the dream-crushing your face to the oneiric earth and burying you in the utopian furrow, run and be the spit you spit in your face, run. Kai Bredholt runs with the block of ice in his arms. He runs, and invisible creatures spit in his face with invisible spit, and he runs: this is the sequence Eugenio Barba chooses.

Let's make love in the earth-cemetery. And be careful not to change it. Let's make love with our memories. And be careful not to crease them. Let's make love in the bed-coffin. And be careful not to dirty its sheet.

After we have made love, we need to carefully hang the suit-remembrance on the wall pin. Tomorrow we shall make love again.

Spinning within the sphere.

The Rock Musician – a spectral Don Juan pursuing voluptuous love, craving to possess the woman he looks for in every woman.

The Rumanian Housewife, down on her knees, wipes and wipes and sings: „Ce chip are tatăl tău / Adevărați sunt tații toți / În adâncul lacului el zace / Și pe el, mai ales, l-ar pescui / Peștii i-au lăsat doar oasele", "What is your father's face like / All fathers are true / He lies at the bottom of the lake / And it is him one should fish / The fish left only his bones", a song-prayer which burns in the Romanian language.

Giddy-up, horse! Giddy-up! So what if you are made out of wood? Come, let me swing. And, then, let's fly. Do you want us to? Giddy-up!

In the beginning, you are beautiful and pure. As time goes by, you lose a leg and keep the other leg in the shopping bag.

Coin, puppet, candle, sheet, helmet, wing, ice, card, plate, spoon, gun, bag, cloth, bread, key, door, sword, handkerchief, crate, tablecloth, suit, flag, garland, pan, bridal veil, watercolour, book, stone, guitar, belt, mirror, leash, television.

The *wild* man can reach self-fulfilment if he is *tamed*, not *domesticated*.

The sacred value of the Black Madonna's words is contained in the mantra 'OM' and in her actions which sometimes are marked by poetic justice: to tear the card which shows someone's destiny into pieces, to smash the door made out of cards, to stab the suit which is a reminder of the past.

And the only character who acts like a fish letting herself caught on a hook is the Rumanian Housewife.

The moment the Puppet holds a card in his little hand, he resembles Scheherezade in *Andersen's Dream*.

Sublime simultaneities: swirls of sword and cards which cry and white spots under feet slipping and dance and loneliness and he is with himself and she is with herself and silhouettes turning their heads and eyes watching the other and reading his destiny and key knocked onto the floor and the dance of the divinity and the wings twisting in flight and the door to paradise: *e la nave va,* buon viaggio!

The translucence of the coffin-aquarium, the translucence of the nylon bag and the translucence of the plastic suit bag.

The Christic image: the Black Madonna, the Rumanian Housewife, the Puppet hanging on hooks with the arms outstretched.

"I asked myself, looking for an answer in action, how I could create a profoundly individualistic theatre, rooted in the most intimate necessity and representing a form of rejection of the surrounding norms of the time. Was it possible, through theatre, to follow the example of Renan's nihilist, Christ?" (Barba 1999a: 104)

The Rumanian Housewife stuffs bread into the Young Colombian's mouth the same way Messer, in *Brecht's Ashes,* stuffs the copy of *Pravda* into Kattrin's mouth.

Sudden changes from actions tinged with the sacred to domestic actions.

Eugenio Barba rehearses a sequence with which the performance might end: the Black Madonna shoots an arrow to open a tunnel of light.

Perceptions depend directly on the forcefulness and profoundness of the thought.

The thought hunts the thoughts.

Chiudi la porta! / *Close the door*! / *Închide ușa*! you shout while you open the door.

Cards thrown in the air during the march of the losers, the crippled, of those stuck in the past, in the mirage of happiness, in the fugitive illusion, in the triumph of the ashes, in the glory of the fools; dissimulation, confetti, the fanfare of the wounded, the shrieks and the cannon fire of the desperate hailing *the brave new world*!

"A precise ritual as a mathematical formula. In the centre an empty throne. For the spectator." (Barba 2012a: 145)

Friday, 11 February 2011, Holstebro

A cry of cardboard

What is a meal you eat without being hungry? A coffin. What is a bed when you do not have a sweet sleep to hold you tight till dawn? A coffin. What is a door which does not open when you knock at it? A coffin.

What is a ladder you climb only to go down? A coffin. What is a journey to a new place where you realise that *you have taken yourself with you*? A coffin. What is an altar to whom you pray without faith? A coffin. What is the sky you look at without seeing the stars behind the clouds? A coffin. Who are you without the *real* you? A coffin. What is life without love? A coffin. And on a coffin, you have sex with death for your lover is dead and it is only his suit you hold now in your arms. It is only you to animate it. The suit? A cloth you carry with you, in you; a cloth-thief for it took the place of your soul. And as you have been having sex on the coffin for so many years, you have got tired and no longer hug the suit passionately, feverishly, lustfully; yes, you have got tired; your cheeks are no longer flushed with excitement; lifeless lover; lifeless suit; lifeless embrace; only you struggling to love him now the same way you loved him once; you kneeling by the coffin of your lover; you forcing yourself to cry; not a tear runs down your face; and then because you want by all means to cry, you pretend to cry; pretend to suffer; you give moans of despair; faked moans of faked despair; faked cry; a cry of cardboard, a cry of cards.

Monday, 14 February 2011, Holstebro

Searches go on

În-chi-de u-șa (*Close the door*), I hear Eugenio Barba saying and, taken by surprise, I hiccup.

I quickly note down the director's observations on the different modes of animating the Puppet, on the technical possibilities of suspending him from hooks and on the changes of the scenic space. He intends to replace Lolito with a new Puppet, his future twin. Then, he starts working, in detail, on the sequence between Tage Larsen, his gesture of gently hitting the table with the corner of his coat is of delightful humour, and the bohemian Jan Ferslev. The next sequence he works on is that of Roberta Carreri, in which he refines the actions she performs to suffocate herself with the bag. While watching them rehearsing, I feel shivers up and down the back of my neck. It is absolutely fantastic! I am so captivated by the micro-scenes in which the actress, sometimes longing for warmth and tenderness, waiting to be caressed, cries with pleasure and sometimes, crinkling her skirt with nervous fingers, slightly trembles. Her icy shivers of death, her mute desperation go straight to the essence of human suffering. In the following micro-scenes, he focuses his attention on Bredholt's shamanic spin and Rasmussen's dancing fingers; the scenes make me think of the fragile thread between life and death: the ardent embrace of love versus the cold embrace of death.

> *Smettila di cercare tuo padre / Stop searching for your father*
> Living opposites: speaking out the truth and lying, eating and spitting, loving and dying.
> Disturbing dream?
> Bad story ending?
> Marriage in death?

Barba works on the sequence with the song *Vaca loca (mad cow)*: all actors sing as they dance in circle; the director explores the different qualities of vocal and body rhythms while he weaves vocal with physical actions.

My eyes linger on the interior of the room inhabited by the Chechnyan Refugee: two cards, King and Queen of Hearts; a painting showing a bridge over a river; lilies of the valley pinned on the top of the wall; a rose hidden in a bride's veil hanging from a hook; two pans, again flowers, this time in a chest. Are they flowers blooming in the morning? Sprinkled with dew? No; they are plastic flowers. So! What does her paradise look like? Garlands and pans! A plastic place embellished with plastic flowers. Luckily, they do not need to be watered.

Wednesday, 16 February 2011, Holstebro

A Tower of Babel

It is the morning Eugenio Barba looks for different spots to place the television, discusses different possible images which might run on the screen, works with the actors on the sequence which I entitled *Stand by Your Man*.

Then, in the first scene, he introduces a card and a pistol wrapped in a white cloth and tied with a black string: the Widow of a Basque Officer shows the card to the Young Colombian and with his forefinger points to the gun; so, from the beginning of the performance, the spectator notices the presence of two symbolic objects: the card of destiny and the murder weapon; at the end of the performance, the Young Colombian, after he comes out of the coffin, pulls out the gun intending to direct it at his twin, the Italian Violinist, but suddenly renounces; there is no need to defend himself as there is no need to commit murder.

Everything is in a heartbeat: in systole and diastole.

The Chechnyan Refugee, decorating her room, believes that she will finally breathe the air of love. But what kind of love is provided by photographs hanging on walls, by images coming out from the mouth of television? It is a marriage with her memories. And it is also a technological marriage: between herself and her beloved television.

However, while she is busy ornamenting the space, the Black Madonna throws confetti, the Danish Lawyer recites pathetically, the Rumanian Housewife and the Rock Musician sing and dance sensually, the Young Colombian sleeps in the coffin. Different scenes, apparently disconnected, are performed simultaneously: one decorates a room, one plays cards, one throws confetti, one sings, one sleeps; all this while the actors speak in different languages reminding me of the Tower of Babel.

And it is as if coins like tears fall out of the tower's windows.

Thursday, 17 February 2011, Holstebro

The body poetry

"I wanted to keep dancing but God said to me: It's Enough. I stopped. I felt the presence of God. He loved me. I loved him. We were married. Today was the day of my marriage with God." (Nagel Rasmussen 1984: 9-10)

Iben Nagel Rasmussen and the Black Madonna: the actress, with a profound, mysterious voice, chants incantations like a witch who does not make *the fire burn and cauldron bubble* (Shakespeare 2005: 109) foretelling Macbeth's tragic destiny, but reads the destinies of ordinary people in the playing cards. Puff!, she throws the cards in the air and her action seems to tell the spectators that it is all for naught. It is the husky quality of her voice, when she whispers, that still echoes in my ears. It is the image of her shadowy body leaving behind a trace of luminous smoke that still haunts me. And it is her last farewell to the Puppet, her wail, her incantation, her singing, her spectral appearance, that is her scenic presence resembling *the extraordinary presence of a samurai* (Carreri 2007: 40) that I will never forget.

Through her dreamlike actions, beautiful and grotesque, the actress brings a past of endless sacrifices into the present. Her gestures seem to evoke forgotten gestures of archaic forgotten rituals. Perfectly mastering her body and voice, the actress tells the spectator the story of the "body poetry" (Nagel Rasmussen 2018: 350), of its shades and scents. When crouching in the shadows, her body seems to slowly melt.

Three small hands, *symbols of the abuse of power in* The Gospel according to Oxyrhincus *that proliferated in* Mythos *as severed hands which materialised the horror from which the spirit of the time averted its gaze, worn out by the will to change the world* (Barba 2010a: 171) form the Black Madonna's crown, in *The Chronic Life*, a performance that undoubtedly speaks about *the mutilated human integrity* (Nagel Rasmussen 2018: 213). Three small hands which reign over the unhappy lives of the little ones.

At the end of the performance, the Black Madonna appears as a vulnerable being walking with shaky steps, her emptied-eyes turned to the edge of a horizon she no longer sees; a blind creature sliding on the surface of a reality she can no longer understand. The gaze of an old, feeble woman with her mind stuck in the memories of the past, of the bitter experiences she has gone through. A ghostly figure, groping in full light, attracted to the coffin against her will, a body decomposing with every step that carries her to the grave. Her unreal presence evokes the image of the Shaman in *Come! And the Day Will Be Ours*: "humiliated and stripped of his ritual garments, his spirit-evoking drum and his necklace" (Nagel Rasmussen 2018: 121).

Still, paradoxically, the Black Madonna, as the Shaman *holds onto the essential: her identity through song* (Nagel Rasmussen 2018: 121).

Her "transparent body" (Nagel Rasmussen 2018: 347) in *Itsi-Bitsi, White as Jasmine, Inside the Skeleton of the Whale, Ode to Progress, Ester's Book, The Chronic Life* haunts the spectator's memories for a long time. A haunting, perhaps resembling one of Iben Nagel Rasmussen's dreams, in which *characters, costumes and situations mix together* (Nagel Rasmussen 2000: 135) and whose oniric logic she put to use in preparation for the performance *Itsi-Bitsi*.

The secret garden of the actor

"Over time, I acquired the capacity *to think with my body*, that is to translate instantly the intentions into actions." (Carreri 2007: 177)

Roberta Carreri and the Rumanian Housewife: a queen of the stage, an actress with a volcanic temperament, who is in perfect symbiosis with her character. On the sequence *Vaca loca*, taking the magic baton of the conductor, she leads the actors-orchestra with her heart. I remember her eyes flickering with an intense passion while longing to suffocate herself with a plastic bag, burying her crying face in the kitchen cloth, swallowing, spitting and vomiting. Her body *in tension* reaches peaks of perfection in moments of sadness, tiredness, sleepiness, deadness, inexorable falls into the void. Her actions, splendidly refined, are performed with the ultimate of rigour and precision, attention being paid to the tiniest detail. Her walking, running, crawling, flying, smiling, laughing, weeping seem to be coloured in shades of sky blue, as the wings of an angel apparently grow from her shoulders, like *branches that hurt*. Every step, every word, every action, executed with mathematical exactness, reveal the perfect coexistence of preciseness and spontaneity. Her scenic presence evokes the force and magnetism of a *wild animal* hypnotising the spectators. When trampling on a castle made out of paper/playing cards, her movements resemble those of a giant animal. The micro-scenes in which she is like a weak animal caught in a trap, a fragile being babbling for she feels alone in the dark, are of a rare beauty. Obsessed with death, she attempts suicide, but each time she attempts, she fails, as she feels too tired to commit it. When she looks into the mirror, all she sees is her ghostly face. At times, lacking the concreteness of a human being, The Rumanian Housewife seems to be a phantom doomed to endlessly wipe the walls of a house also doomed to exist forever. Her heavy blue wings do not let her fly up to the sky; her tormented tired soul cannot help her escape her nightmares. Suicide remains a sweet dream she cannot make come true.

The Rumanian Housewife reminds me of Antigone in *The Gospel according to Oxyrhincus*:

> "One dies because one does not want,
> One does not want because one thinks one possesses,
> One thinks one possesses because one does not try to give,
> Trying to give, one discovers that one possesses nothing.
> Discovering that one possesses nothing, one tries to give oneself,
> Trying to give oneself, one discovers that one is nothing,
> Discovering that one is nothing, one wants to become,
> Wanting to become, one lives." (Barba 1985a: 75)

My Father's House, Roberta Carreri's first Odin Teatret production that she sees in the spring of 1973, impresses her so strongly that, after the performance, she cries on and on, overwhelmed with the emotions stirred by *so much force, so much beauty, so much life in the seven actors' radiant bodies* (Carreri 2007: 21). The actress notes down: *A daisy between toes. A voice and a name: Fyodor Dostoyevsky. Then the music of an accordion. Dances. Stink. Darkness. Silence. Voices* (Carreri 2007: 20). And her emotions carry her back into her childhood, years of beauty and innocence, when *men lived the code of honour motivating them to become the best they could be* (Carreri 2007: 21). The performance unleashes Carreri's desire to play, to actualise her creative potential, to create characters that speak about love, honour, dignity, friendship, generosity, joy, happiness, passion, courage, deception, degradation, illusion, loneliness, sadness, blindness, dehumanisation.

Roberta Carreri's exceptional scenic presence radiates in her performances and work demonstrations such as *Anabasis, The Million, Brecht's Ashes, The Gospel according to Oxyrhincus, Judith, Inside the Skeleton of the Whale, Salt, Traces in the Snow*, which are true *tours de force*. The quality of her movements and the rigour of her actions are the remarkable achievements of her personal research as well as of the training she does daily to bring her work to perfection. The transition from Geronimo, "born of a costume and nostalgia for absolute innocence" (Carreri 2007: 62), to the Rumanian Housewife consists of numerous scenic metamorphoses of the actress who tells us: "I am a statue that undergoes various metamorphoses while moving to conquer new positions" (Carreri 2007: 55).

"You are in the king's garden. You are afraid, but somebody reaches a hand towards you" (Barba 2010a: 63) is the first improvisation Eugenio Barba gives to Roberta Carreri who, closing her eyes, starts to move slowly through the space. If she had repeated the same improvisation years later, in the light of her experience, she would have followed *the logic in jumps of the associations allowing her to continually re-act to the actions she executes* (Carreri 2007: 100), and then her improvisation would have been like this: *No one is allowed to enter the king's garden ... I should not be here ... I have to be careful not to make noise, not to be noticed ... When I see a beautiful flower and I want to pick it up, I have to be sure that no one sees me ... And when I get it closer to my face, to feel its scent ... hundreds of small warriors jump out of the flower and hit me with their swords ... They start jumping out of all the other flowers! And they hurt me. But it starts raining, and every drop of rain is a little angel whose large wings crush the little warriors ... And so the rain saves me ...* (Carreri 2007: 100).

At the beginning of her career she walked on *the street of her apprenticeship, paved with physical pain and tears of helplessness* (Carreri 2007: 176). During rehearsals I've seen an exceptional actress who radiates the *pleasure of play* intensified in *moments of crisis, growth, change*. For Roberta Carreri, training is a *modus vivendi*, a space and a time *for dialoguing with her craft, not letting herself be swallowed by routine, not losing her 'amazement'* (Carreri 2007: 177-178).

In today's rehearsal, the actors move as if they swim in the sand waves of a desert: their movements resemble those performed by a shaman in a ceremonial dance to invoke the rain; a dance which, at the same time, appears as an incessant struggle with themselves, with the others, and with the *above;* a struggle not to let themselves be swallowed by the desert sands.

In a world governed by words that are not followed by actions, or that often are nothing more than lies used to manipulate others, in Eugenio Barba's dramaturgy, the words are actions and actions tell ancient and contemporary mythical stories, speaking about "events that occurred in different times and places, but, like different rivers, they flow into the same sea" (Carreri 2002: 8).

The new Puppet, Lolito's twin, comes into play.

Friday, 18 February 2011, Holstebro

My ideal was a butterfly (Varley 2011a: 85)

Julia Varley and the Chechnyan Refugee: the actress conceives a playful, dynamic scenic presence. In the process of creating her character, she *concentrated on slightly slowing down her tempo, avoiding underlining the end of an action, while, at the same time, she continuously added tiny variations and brief pauses to diversify each phase of a gesture* (Varley 2011b: 53). Her scenic actions, which are of utmost precision, remind me of her reflections on the actor's dramaturgy: "A body that is whole with its voice dances, thinks and sings while it walks, acts and speaks. [...] In a whole body the voice is synchronised with the physical actions. This does not mean that each word has to have a corresponding action, but that my voice is in harmony with my body as when I dance to a rhythm, in dialogue with it or making counterpoints. It is as if my voice dances to the music of my body's actions, so that they become one. The physical and vocal actions interact like two simultaneous musical scores in the same composition" (Varley 2011a: 40-41).

Doña Musica's Butterflies and The Chronic Life

In *Doña Musica's Butterflies*, Julia Varley operates a double distancing from her character and herself as actress proposing a philosophical meditation on the human condition. The conception of *life as a dream*, and the idea that *life is but a walking shadow* (Shakespeare), or a fragile thread that breaks easily, are embedded in a performance that makes the spectator ask himself questions about the sense of human existence, re-evaluate his life, reflect upon death. In *The Chronic Life,* Julia Varley's reaction to the idea of *creating a funeral ceremony* takes the form of a protest based on disagreement with the director's proposal. Furthermore, she decides to make her appearance in rehearsal as "a man with a moustache [...] allowed to make all kinds of comments" Varley 2011b: 41). So, her personal approach is opposed to the director's initial idea "to create a funeral ceremony with restrained and non-theatrical actions" (Varley 2011b: 42). If in *Doña Musica's Butterflies,* the actress's vocal-physical actions, marked by sobriety, speak about the unforgiving death that lurks in the darkness of our life, in *The Chronic Life,* her scenic actions reveal her determination to achieve her goals; sometimes, while she moves through the space, a determined air emanates from her slightly bent body. If in *Doña Musica's Butterflies,* the actress moves majestically through a circular performance space, delineated by white ropes and flowers, symbolising *the eternal cycle of life and death,* in *The Chronic Life,* her walk, "with arms held parallel and a slightly bouncing step" (Varley 2011b: 41), makes the spectator reflect on the risible dimension of human behaviour. And if in *Doña Musica's Butterflies,* the references to Kafka's parable, *Before the Law,* make visible both the tragic and comic aspects of reality, in *The Chronic Life,* the image of the aquarelle hung on the wooden wall persists in my mind. The thought that I will be for ever prisoner in this deadly Wonderland haunts me. I cannot get rid of this thought not even when the actress leaves the stage playing with a butterfly.

Butterfly? A being whose wings can be easily torn. Our wings are the wings of a butterfly.

Monday, 21 February 2011, Holstebro

The man-bag

Sounds-actions-props: the sound of the spoon hitting on the plate; creeping footsteps; the murder weapon on the table; dimly lit corners; the pistol hanging on a hook; suicide / thought-drug; no one can escape death; never being hungry, never being thirsty, never going anywhere; always silent; the breathing pages of a book; knocks on the metal chest, knocks on the floor, knocks at the door; duduk; the obstacle and the threshold; the spitting of bread; the reddish sword blade; the sharp blades of the scissors; dance-spin-fall-dance; sounds of heaven; laughing and crying; the Black Madonna neighs riding the little wooden horse; melting icicles; the man-bag.

A vocal action replaces a physical action and a stare is the equivalent of a piece of dialogue (Barba 2010a: 25).

Eugenio Barba repeats with Iben Nagel Rasmussen the sequence in which the actress, illuminated by a strip of light, walks through the space. Then, he fixes, with utmost precision, Julia Varley's actions in the micro-sequence she shows the cards to the spectators; "Sfrutta le ombre! / Use the shadows!", he exclaims.

Suddenly there is a strange sound of a key scratching and hitting the door. Unexpectedly, I hear Eugenio Barba speaking Romanian: "Am două chei / I have two keys".

Wednesday, 2 March 2011, Holstebro

Shards of a broken mirror

Red walls, white shrouds; streaks of light springing from the holes in the wooden wall; red light glowing above the black curtain and beneath the spectator's benches; it is the director who creates countless perspectives leading to the apparition of myriads of Lilliputian worlds, changing the face of the performance; the mirror of the Wonderland broken into thousands of pieces reflects a realm of dreams, phantoms, tinged with surrealism; at times, the actors' actions bearing the imprint of magical realism are performed at a dizzying rhythm; flashes of primitive instincts, actions-incursions into the unconscious, seconds of somnambulism, moments of entering and coming out of a trance state; an inward-looking; glittering shards of a broken mirror; and sounds: the sound of a hammer blow, Thor's hammer, screams, whispers, incantatory sounds, magical sounds; an infinity of sounds: the sound of fire, of ice, of swallow, of spit, of vomit, of pacing up and down; the bittersweet sound, the sound that hurts and the sound that caresses, the sound of love; the sound of mirror breaking.

Maya's veil

A corpse covered in a blanket of snow lies on the ground. A corpse like any other corpse. A dead puppet. Maya's veil, kissing for the last time the mouth of the dead, rises gently.

The Black Madonna throws the playing cards foretelling the future.
The black gun sleeps on a corner of the table-bed-coffin.
The heart beats at the same rhythm.
The first voice: "I have washed five men in my life. Five dead men that I loved. I never got married again."
Ice glinting in the blue light.
The war of the big ones – the play of the little ones: riding wooden horses, waving paper swords plus battle cries.
Someone helps you.
The second voice: "This is the key to the door. Behind it you will find your father."
The third voice: "In vain. Stop searching for your father."
Love of the mighty opposites.
All alone even when chained to your lover.
Trapped in your loneliness.
Can you escape the prison of your mind?
You do not integrate, you die or you do not integrate, you live.
The key was forgotten in the door lock.
How to open a locked door without a key.
Silent singing.
Carnival.
The butterfly of the craft.
Red and white tapes marking the crime scene.
Conflict: hate – love / war – art / weapon – violin / violence – kindness.
Travelling across the kingdom of *nowhere*.
There is nothing behind the door.
Torgeir Wethal about Eugenio Barba: "A new performance haunts. I know that it has been turning over in Eugenio's head for a long time. You can tell by what interests him, by listening to what he tells those who come to his lectures, or from conversations with his friends. Fermenting

underneath all this are the things which worry him, both in the distant world and close at hand, his obsessions, his daily qualms for our future (that of the Odin), dreams and memories from his youth, an old man's insight and struggles, professional challenges such as the physical age of his actors, the desire to destroy everything and rebuild from zero, the temptation to slam the door and say: 'Enough!' But he is also aware that someone must continue to open the door to those who knock. What do I know, after all, of what is stirring inside him?" (Rasmussen 2018: 222-223)

Hope

The Chronic Life is conceived as a dream, and in dream the impossible becomes possible: the bed is a coffin, and the coffin is a bed on which you lie down and fall asleep and dream: you dream you die and come back to life; and when you wake up, you step out of the coffin eager to meet your other half. Tell me a dream, the rest is silence.

During the last rehearsals, swarms of thoughts spring up from my mind. Here are some of them:

Icy flowers. A crime scene. Another criminal act in an endless repetition of the first criminal act. The act of killing. To kill seems to be so easy. To use brightly coloured barrier tape to isolate and preserve the crime scene seems to be so easy. Nobody cares that a human being lies on the ground, perhaps a humble human being, who was hunted down. A dead animal in a pen is all that is left.

The tempting impulse to rummage in your pockets for the seeds of life to sow them in new lands is nipped in the bud.

We all know that *from the moment we are born we begin to die*. We are born to die. This is the breathing beings' tragedy.

You find out that people usually fail in fulfilling their lives. They fail to live the life they have dreamed of when they were young. Very young. And then, you feel, somewhere deep inside the fear that you, in turn, will fail. Fear of failing. Fear of losing the force to fight. To resist.

You do not know what to do with your life. Others tell you. But what they tell you is not what you want. You try to do what you want but you do not succeed. And then the others tell you that you have to do something else. Doing something else, you feel that your life lost its compass. Even so, you go on doing what you never wanted, never dreamed of doing. You go on spending your life without searching for its possible sense. Or without searching for your possible sense in life. There is no road for you to follow. Because you do not see the sense of any road for you to follow. You feel trapped in a vicious circle. And every evening when you lie down on your bed you are already dead. A breathing corpse. And what hurts, hurts badly, is that the others did not kill your dreams. The others killed in you the will, the courage, the desire to make your dreams come true. And which is your fundamental dream? To be alive. And how can one be alive in the absence of *his* sense of being alive?

At the end of *The Chronic Life*, two young boys follow a path that leads to a door they open with a secret key. Laughing and looking happy, they enter the world behind the door. You want to join them, enter their play in their secret world.

And you hope the play is the play of love.

"Through love, the thorn becomes a rose.
Through love, vinegar becomes sweet wine.
Through love, the pyre becomes a throne.
Through love, rage becomes grace.
Through love, sickness becomes health." (Nagel Rasmussen 1984: 5)

A reversed look

Eugenio Barba, a genius of the *dramaturgy written on stage*, masterfully makes use of *reversals*, simultaneities and coexistences of opposites, inoculating doubt, creating surprise, suspense, ambiguity, *making the invisible visible*.

I take my courage in both hands and try a reading of the performance from the end to the beginning. A reversed look. It is as if I project myself at the end of the tunnel and before I take the last step, I see in my mind's eye life events, *imprinted* in my soul, that unfold backwards. Flashbacks before the final exit.

So, the performance speaks about the past and the future of our world. And because our world, our global community, is made of individuals, we must not forget that every individual has a life of his own and his life is the most precious present given to him, to humanity. But the world is at war and war brings death not life. Some die. Others live hoping they will live forever, not thinking of the day they will also die. However, it is not a matter of dying. We all die in the end. It is a matter of how we live till we die. I repeat: unfortunately, in a state of permanent war. We know: the life choices we make have consequences; it is up to us to decide our personal road; that is why it is essential to listen to our inner voice which tells us to visualise the road before we follow it. Visualising it, we become capable of choosing from the countless future roads the one that changes our lives. The chance to change ourselves is not given to us only once in life. Every moment we have this chance. Some say that at the end of one's life, before crossing the threshold into the realm of the Absolute, there are a few seconds in which one may have the revelation of one's wrong choices. This revelation seems to be similar to the vision of *The Chronic Life*.

At a reversed look, the performance would begin with a boy's awakening into a world he has never been before. It is a strange land whose shores appear to be washed by the dark blue waters of the primordial ocean. Exploring the surroundings, he arrives at an old, beautiful house. He knocks at the door. Nobody answers. But the young boy, unlike the Man from the countryside, opens the door. Getting inside, he sees other doors waiting to be opened. Now he has to make his own choice. Which door will he open? There is a story hidden behind every door. A story to be told or to be kept secret. Which story will he choose? And it would end with the detachment of the soul from the body, a journey of the soul-bird to heaven, a cloud of light floating in the sky.

If I were to write in a sentence what I have thought and felt during the rehearsals for *The Chronic Life*, I would open Boris Vian's beautiful book, *Foam of the Daze*, at page 57: *The Blue room is always full of lilies, white gladiolas, and lots of other white flowers, and, above all, red roses...* (Vian 2003: 57).

Imagine our Father

"But the books which preserve the revolts of the past evoke the spirit of our time. The images in the newspapers are superimposed on the pages of the books." (Barba 1985b: 23)

Perhaps *The Chronic Life* is the tragedy of every yesterday, today and tomorrow. The tragedy man, consciously-unconsciously, lives in, for today, as yesterday and tomorrow, sometimes he crawls like a spineless being doomed to carry his dwelling with him. His muffled cry is heart-wrenching, his dreams are broken and his ideals are shattered. And sometimes, instead of embracing the whole world, he grabs his prey with predatory claws. Instead of running, he limps. Instead of breathing the breath of life, he releases evil onto the earth. Displaying ferocious cruelty, man has turned a deaf ear to his crying victims. At the same time it is the tragedy of man who has lost his hope to meet the other half of his soul, to find absolute love. Man as a whole being has been replaced by the Beckettian mouth which speaks, speaks, speaks. A mouth that takes a hold on him completely and strokes his ego. His mind, body, and soul suffer in sad silence. And it is also the never-ending tragedy of *sick animals* peregrinating all over the world in search of healing and love. The tragedy of man who wrestles with the Angel. The tragedy of man trapped in history. The tragedy of man trapped by his emotions. The tragedy of man manipulated by Iago's lies. The tragedy of man who believes that *failure* is all that has been given to him. The tragedy of man who struggles with / against his deaf ear and his blind eye and his gossiping mouth and his nail-claw and hopes that one day he will find the road to his self. Even though, man has been dying out, at times, in the solitude of night, his inner voice whispers to him the way to fight the evil within himself.

"But in a world where people around us either no longer believe in anything, or only pretend to believe in order to be left in peace, he who digs deep within himself to reach a clarity about his own situation, his absence of certitudes, his need for spiritual life, will always be called fanatic or naive. In a world where cheating is a norm, he who seeks his own truth is taken for a hypocrite." (Barba-D'Urso 2000: 48)

On 5 February 2008, the first day of rehearsals for *The Chronic Life,* Eugenio Barba proposes his own funeral as the theme of the future performance: "One day you come to the theatre and someone tells you that I've died. In a letter I ask you to organise my funeral with what you know I love. You will be able to converse with me, tell me things you have never told me. For so many years you've all struggled against being crushed by the Angel. You must create a scene in which you show the struggle between Jacob and the Angel. Tell a story full of horror and humour, a story about me, in which you must only refer to me as 'him', never 'you'. You must each prepare your own ceremony, in just a few minutes. You decide how" (Carreri 2011: 58). His proposal, the estrangement from one's own funeral as well as from the funeral of the persons one loves, brings to my mind Albert Camus's *The Stranger.* The director's idea implies a return to the past and a visualisation of the future. In a way, inexorably, one's everyday life recurs in the same patterns in the future. But, proposing the theme of his own funeral, Barba breaks the apparently implacable daily ritual; and, all of a sudden, what seems to be inconceivable or distant, that is one's impending death, emerges at the surface and takes shape. At the same time, to foreshadow an unexpected death presupposes to make a retrospective of the past. In this regard, Roberta Carreri remarks: "Now, however, instead of trying to escape from the past, we are to dig up fragments of performances that are now extinct: scenes, costumes, objects, songs" (Carreri 2011: 58). It is a process that requires lucid thinking and sharpening of senses, detachment and dedublation. It is a near-death experience. A travel to the future through the tunnel of memory. An archetypal journey. A ritual of death.

How did the actors react to the theme? How did they feel experiencing a death ritual? Perhaps, at the beginning of the creative process, it was the *Disorder* that manifested itself violently as an *intensified reality, that of the possible disappearance of the beloved one,* came into being. Perhaps Barba's words brought to the actors' minds both dear and regretful memories. Perhaps his words resonating powerfully in their souls reminded them that there is something beyond human power. Perhaps they thought to set their house on fire and build a new one. Perhaps, *struggling against being crushed by the Angel,* their will to live became stronger. Perhaps the actors asked themselves: Why does man die? And because he knows one day he dies, why doesn't he live every day of his life as his last day? And because he is to die, why doesn't he give himself the chance to make the impossible possible? Nevertheless, the actors' struggle on the *Raft of the Medusa* apparently is no longer a matter of *to eat and to be eaten.* It is rather a struggle for each of them with himself/herself to keep under control the avalanche of instincts, emotions and thoughts, to cultivate his/her patience, moral thinking, compassion and tolerance toward his/her fellow sufferers.

At the same time, Barba's proposal makes reference to his *roots*: *1940-1945, times of war, when the houses collapsed under the bombs were shaken by laments, people being buried alive, their cries being heard from under the rubble; his fear not to catch the eel that swam at the bottom of the cistern full of rainwater in the courtyard; if the eel had died, the water would have been undrinkable* (Barba 2010a: 4); *his run to the shop where they sold ice needed to stop his father's haemorrhage; his running carrying the block of ice* (Barba 2010a: 36).

The Widow keeps watch at the bedside of the dying man. As if in a trance, she murmurs words which evoke instants of her life. The words which float down the river of her memories, recall her husband's agony, his last breath, the moment she *opened the window for his soul to fly out.* It is so true that "The *wounds* are stories which do not wish to be told. [...] Perhaps because they know their destiny is elsewhere, to be poured into another story, the smokescreen which allows us to evoke and conceal them at one and the same time" (Barba 2010a: 173). In the process of creating his character, the Widow of a Basque Officer, Kai Bredholt visualises the life of a woman, Donna Vera, Eugenio Barba's mother. The actor *does simple domestic actions such as laying out a tablecloth, setting the table and preparing the bed; the Puppet, placed on the ground, is dressed as in a photograph of Eugenio Barba as a child* (Bredholt 2011: 32). *Traces of autobiography, not of confession* (Barba 2010a: 173) combined with *the shadows of the greater history* are also present in *The Chronic Life.* In this respect, Barba tells us: "My groping work on the evocative dramaturgy meant *unconsciously* invoking in the belly of the performance the shadows of the greater history and the small history from which I came" (Barba 2010a: 189).

From the beginning of the working process, a coffin filled with water in which an eel swims is in the Blue room. The transparent coffin resembling the one from *Snow White* (Carreri 2011: 59) makes the spectator think of *eternal life*. As in a fairy tale, to die is to sleep and dream. But it is only in the fairy tale that love awakens the *sleeping beauty*. Does *The Chronic Life* have a happy ending? Does the Young Colombian enter the realm of love which never dies? I do not know. Perhaps it is *his ignorance* which guides him to *his* door and carries his steps not to a happy ending but toward the beginning of another journey, along which he may repeat the inherent experiences of *the one who does not integrate*. In this sense, the *ignorance* Ernest Renan speaks about in *Life of Jesus* comes to my mind: "Refinement of manners and acuteness of intellect have, in the East, nothing in common with what we call education. It is the men of the schools, on the contrary, who are considered as being pedantic and wanting in manners. In a social state such as this, ignorance, which with us condemns a man to an inferior position, is the condition of great things and of high originality" (Renan 1897: 21). At the end of the performance, the sound of the violin and not that of the gun is heard. It is a play of joy and not a fight of *one against another*. It is all about everlasting love. The music of the spheres replaces the noise of the weapons.

At the outset of the performance journey, Eugenio Barba utters the words: *I came because I was told my father lived here.* It is a sentence from Juan Rulfo's novel, *Pedro Páramo*, which tells *the story of a young man who travels to the place where his mother was born in search of his father and once he is there he is greeted by the ghosts of a bygone life* (Monsalve 2011: 24). It is a key sentence for the Young Colombian character. The character's story, a boy who arrives in a foreign country in search of his father, reminds me of the story of another orphan child: "Once there was a poor child with no mother and no father. Everything was dead and there wasn't a soul left on Earth. Everything was dead and the child went out and searched day and night. But since there was no one left on Earth he wanted to go up to Heaven, and indeed the Moon looked down kindly at him, but when he got up to the Moon it was just a piece of rotten wood. So he set off for the Sun, and when he got there it was only a withered sunflower, and when he got to the stars they were only golden gnats that a shrike had stuck to a black thorn bush, and when the child wanted to go back down to Earth, it was just an upside-down chamber pot and the child was all alone. Then he sat down and cried and he's still sitting there to this day, all alone" (Büchner 2014). Similarly, the Young Colombian knocks at all doors, but all doors seem to be closed. Does he feel the sky falling down on him? Crushing him? Does he feel his feet stuck in the sand? Does he feel as if his soul has been stolen to be taken to Hades? Does he follow a dream thread? The dream of wholeness? Of rediscovering his own identity? Is he predestined to remain for ever hungry? To be endlessly offered empty plates or plates full of coins? There is a micro-scene, which I entitled *the rattling coins and their metallic dance*, in which the boy fed by the Widow swallows metal coins. Obviously, in this *Wonderland,* the poor and helpless child, longing for love and protection, dreams about his last home.

Ferdinando Taviani notices that "the performance begins with a little bit sacred, a little bit farcical, and a little bit savage figure: a Black Madonna who seems to have just descended from the altar, a merciful and ferocious mother with a sword in her heart. She enters the empty space, passes by a corpse on the ground, throws playing cards in the air like a witch. She crouches down and mutters in her own guttural Latin, which resembles the mumble of a man too old to speak or a childish gurgling. Someone sings in falsetto: a tall person, elegantly dressed in black, enters. The person brings in a soup bowl, cutlery and a serviette. The attention shifts to the centre stage where there is a white tablecloth on the table. The tablecloth becomes a sheet. The sheet becomes a shroud. A story, regarding a military father who dies, an orphan and a widow, begins" (Barba 2012a: IV). So, in what kind of world does the Black Madonna throw cards in the air? In a world where the Young Colombian, in search for his father, comes to be buried under a table around which characters sit playing cards and utter apathetically the names of those who have passed away, victims of war, of indifference, of intolerance, of selfishness, names they evoke *en passant* being totally engaged in their play. In a world where no matter how frenziedly the Rumanian Housewife cleans, she cannot remove the dirt. A world impossible to purify. A world called Wonderland in which the boy does *not integrate*. How ironically and bitterly the word "Wonderland" sounds! The Young Colombian is still a child and therefore *the kingdom of God belongs to him: one is or one must become a child to enter therein, one ought to receive it as a child; the heavenly Father hides his secrets from the wise and reveals them to little ones* (Renan 1897: 122). His search for his father is at the same time an ideal. Ernest Renan's reflection upon ideal springs to mind: "Essentially the ideal is ever a Utopia. [...] The new earth, the new heaven, the new Jerusalem descending from above, the cry: 'Behold I make all things new!' are characteristics common to all reformers. The contrast of the ideal with the pitiful reality will always cause human revolts against dispassionate reason such as these, which the man of petty mind regards as madness until the day of their triumph, when those who have opposed them will be the first to recognise their reasonableness" (Renan 1897: 80-81).

The destiny of the Young Colombian: The Road to Golgotha? The Resurrection?

"A man's name is the essence of his being. God's names are the essence of the Mystery of Life" (Barba 1985a: 45). But the characters in *The Chronic Life* have no names. The divinity to whom they pray is a bivalent, Eurasian divinity, Madonna and Kali.

And I think it is we who crush the heart of heaven under our feet; it is we who turn everything into dust; it is we who, possessed by belligerent desires, fight doggedly against the others; it is we who eradicate the mystery of life and transform the divinity into a carnivalesque, ridiculous figure; it is we who limping throw confetti with satisfied smiles on our faces in a pathetic atmosphere of celebration. In a *vanity fair* our sadness and loneliness are intensified by the absence of the Father. Our bandaged wounds incessantly bleed. Our compass is broken. And we do not know where to go. The others, willingly or not, always point us in the wrong direction, making us feel stuck on the road. Going without going anywhere. But despite all this, we hope to live the transition *from fact to legend* (Barba 2010a: XI). We hope that our beautiful naivety, passionate love and ideals never fade. For instance, the ideal of shared love. For "Who are we, we humans, who can conceive the idea of God and yet be so inhuman with our fellow men; we who can laugh while in pain and cry with joy" (Carreri 2011: 65-66). Who are we? It is we who are buried in the house of the soulless beings hunted/haunted by The Other / Others: *I am a gaze observing you, a formless thought that thinks you* (Sartre 1989: 44) [...] *I'm watching you, everybody's watching, I'm a crowd all by myself* and yes *this is hell, hell is other people* (Sartre 1989: 45). It is we who want to have an adorable gingerbread house without knowing that it is inhabited by ancestral criminal instincts. It is we who live in the house of our illusions which sicken and devour us: *I could turn this place into a penthouse, for instance, this room you could have as the kitchen, yes, I'd have teal-blue, copper and parchment linoleum squares, you could put the dining-room across the landing, yes, Venetian blinds on the window, cork floor, cork tiles, an off-white pile linen rug, a table in afromosia teak veneer, sideboard with matt black drawers, curved chairs with cushioned seats, armchairs in oatmeal tweed, a beech frame settee with a woven sea-grass seat, white-topped heat-resistant coffee table, white tile surround, yes, and then the bedroom, the bedroom-a retreat, furniture ... mahogany and rosewood, deep azure-blue carpet, unglazed blue and white curtains, a bedspread with a pattern of small blue roses on a white ground ... it wouldn't be a flat it'd be a palace* (Pinter 1971: 60).

It is we who think: "One always dies too soon – or too late. And yet one's whole life is complete at that moment, with a line drawn neatly under it, ready for the summing up. You are – your life" (Sartre 1989: 43). You are your house. It is we who think of the *house built from living stones*, of the mosque and of the stupa. It is we who think of the house which is neither a building nor a gathering, neither a group nor an organisation. Every human being is the house in which his soul lives.

It is we who think of the house of evil thoughts: "For from within, out of the heart of men, proceed evil thoughts, adulteries, fornications, murders, / thefts, covetousness, wickedness, deceit, lasciviousness, an evil eye, blasphemy, pride, foolishness: / All these evil things come from within, and defile the man" (Mark 7. 21-23).

And it is we who think of the house of theatre: *I think of some old poor houses in the southern countries; in every house there is a small ladder, blackened by time, leading to the flat roof where you can lie down, look at the sky, talk to yourself, with your gaze lost somewhere over the horizon. For me, theatre is similar to this house* (Barba 2010b: 95).

It is we who think of the house of man for "God dwells in man, and lives by man, even as man dwells in God, and lives by God" (Renan 1897: 154). And it is we who think of the house of superman as well.

Who are we who think of all this? Perhaps our search for father is to imagine our Father. Perhaps. I do not know.

Even now I hear the Rumanian Housewife shouting: "Închide uşa! Închide uşa! Închide uşa!" Shut the door! Is the door shut? No. The door is and will always be open, for the search of our Father is never-ending.

The words *iş-işa-uşa* are still alive in me.

Welcome home!

Welcome home!

Dare enter the houses destroyed by war! Enjoy ourselves! Enter the time of the abandoned children! Lovely! The era of the great evil! Our era! God left and never returned! Splendid! Let's all sing the song of war! War! War! War! We want war! Out with the small war! In with the big war! Out with the world war! In with the galactic war! It is time to make a new deal with the devil! He gives us absolute power! We offer him human souls! Victory will be ours! Ram-pam-pam! Pam-pam! Enjoy-joy-enjoy! Perfect! Now let's execute all our enemies! One by one! Kill them slowly or kill them quickly! It does not matter! Kill them all! All! All! All! Adieu! Enjoy the Satan's fire! Yes! Enjoy the smell of our enemies' blood! Yes! Pa-rampam-pam! Yes! Yes! What? I repeat! God does not exist! I repeat! God is dead! Dead! Love? Bleahhh! Love does not exist! Love is dead! I repeat! Man is not the house of God! Man is the tower of Lucifer! Send all love to the recycle bin! Hip-hip-hurrah! The past stinks! Send the past to the recycle bin! Enjoy the bloody future! Build robot armies! Houses on Mars! Swimming pools on Saturn! Hip-hip-hurrah! Get a knife, cut your heart out and replace it with an electric heart! Electric! Have electric sex on purple sheets whenever you want! When in need of sex, connect yourselves! When tired of so much sex, disconnect yourselves! I repeat! Tenderness and kindness stink! Send them to the recycle bin! I repeat: Forget about Father! The stubborn ones who insist on searching for their Father belong to the past and will be put to death! Hip-hip-hurrah! Long live the electric-man! Pam-pam!

As in a dream, I glimpse *images of a galactic war, of a desperate passion, of a sense of honour and a contempt for life, of a tenderness for the madness and the weakness of human beings crushed by the ferocity of history* (Barba 1999a: 15).

Welcome home!

Let us whip ourselves till the blood comes in streams / till we exorcise the guilt we feel for our sins: "Open the door! Open, blast you! I'll endure anything, your red-hot tongs and molten lead, your racks and prongs and garrottes – all your fiendish gadgets, everything that burns and flays and tears – I'll put up with any torture you impose. Anything, anything would be better than this agony of mind, this creeping pain that gnaws and fumbles and caresses one and never hurts quite enough" (Sartre 1989: 41).

Today, Monday, 7 February 2011, I say today because tomorrow Eugenio Barba might change the order of the scenes, so, today it all begins when the Rock Musician enters the space, and when he gets near the table instantly starts screaming and whipping the table in a fit of madness. Crippled with guilt and remorse, he enters staggering, with a hunted look on his spectral face as if summoned to appear in court to be sentenced to life imprisonment, but while he nears the table covered with vividly coloured cloths, he straightens his body and walks steadily. An unstoppable desire to punish himself takes hold of him. The space smells of burning candles, blind rebellion and misery. With a sudden gesture he whips savagely the table and himself and his hysteria reaches an incredible crescendo. He hits and hits and hits, blinded by passion, feeling the impulsive desire to put an end to his unbearable life. I imagine his parents wanted him to have a great destiny, but life mocked him and, in time, his illusions shattered. Alas, illusions are just illusions. No more than that. So he tries to destroy both everything that surrounds him and himself. When the candles burn out, groping in the dark, he searches for the light. But there is no light. It is only he staring into the emptiness. *Let there be light!*, I am on the point of screaming when I see him whipping himself again. Punishment and self-punishment.

Cin-cin, let's drink, *for fear of death urges us to endlessly repeat the games of death on beds of love!* (Marinetti)

Home: a place you find after an exhausting search through the dark corridors of history: *the small and big Histories. A story line:* "how does a person become integrated? We have Julia's [Varley] character who allows herself to be integrated, and Sofia's [Monsalve] who refuses to be integrated" (Carreri 2011: 64). *Uprooting*: everybody plays a role: of mother and father at the same time, of a goddess of war / protectress of the wounded soldier on the battlefield, of Don Juan, of a housewife whose destiny resembles that of Medea's as an anonymous being, named Sugar, may suffer a terrible destiny similar to that of a queen or of those few who have the courage to follow their destinies imprinting deep traces in the collective memory, in the big history of the world.

Welcome home!

Chew, chew, chew and spit out!

My character has a destiny no less than the one of Medea's, Roberta Carreri tells the participants in the programme *The Collective Mind*, Wrocław, 2010.

Her character is a victim of *violence and abuse*. A heroine of our times whose *story is tragic and banal at the same time*: "The tragedy of everyday life, or the everyday nature of tragedy? How many women with tragic destinies serve us coffee with a smile?" (Carreri 2011: 61)

I see in the Rumanian Housewife an ordinary woman in desperate need of love and kindness in her life. Perhaps she felt suffocated by her partner and left him. Perhaps she hates her work but she is incapable of overcoming her social condition. I think, every morning, she feels tired, too tired to continue with her miserable life. She is a beautiful woman who stuffs her mouth with bread which she cannot swallow and spits it out. A woman who dreams of a beautiful life. A woman who wishes to experience *a little death*, to immerse herself in love. A woman who falls into states of trance, her soul flying freely through the heavens. A woman-angel with turquoise wings: "between animal and angel [...] she, my adored one, though all body, was a chaster body, untainted by humanity, and stood much closer to the angels" (Mann 1955: 207).

And, sometimes, while she cleans the house, she dreams with her eyes wide open of the starry nights and the sweet song of the nightingale. And when she wipes the floor she gives me the impression that she is trying to clean up her entire life. And when she throws herself into her lover's arms passionately, it is as if the whole world sings with joy. And, sometimes, she bursts into hysterical laughter and screams when she is taken by surprise. And, sometimes, her body suspended from a hook looks like a dead swan. And, sometimes, blindfolded she crawls on the floor singing a song about death. And, sometimes, with a tender, sweet gesture she puts flowers on the coffin. And, sometimes, trembling with repulsion as if she has dragged her body through garbage and dirty dishes, sliding on her knees, she wipes the dirt off the floor surface; she bites the bread and spits it, dirties the place with spittle and chewed-unchewed bread, and all of a sudden she starts gathering the rubbish cleaning her house till it shines. And when the candle burns out, it seems that the housewife is guarded by a beautiful, blue angel.

A *dance of the intentions* (Carreri 2007: 88) turned into a *dance of the fallen angel*.

Welcome home!

What about the *emigrant* condition? Let's speculate on it!

A guy flirts with you, takes off his jacket and puts it on you to make you feel warmer, helps you cross a rivulet, tells you that happiness waits for you in Wonderland, promises to take you there, and you believe him although right from the start you could have noticed that your guy holds a book in one hand and a stone in the other. So, you follow him even when the guy nonchalantly takes his jacket back. Well, life is not a beautiful dream, people do bad things and refuse to help others mainly because they are not capable of helping themselves.

The Chechnyan Refugee makes her appearance into the so-called New World crawling from behind a black curtain. I imagine she appears from the darkness which mantles the place she escapes from. At first, I see a hand pushing forward a green metal crate, then a body that sneaks into the scenic space. An illegal entry. Uprootedness, exile, yearning for freedom?

She does not encounter any difficulty in crossing the border and she will not be expelled as she gets herself a passport. Once she is in, she displays her colourful tablecloths, grieves pathetically her lost husband, caressing his suit from time to time, and hangs her pans, family photos and watercolours proudly on the wooden wall. Decorating her new home with plastic grape leaves, she believes herself happy but she is mistaken. She finds neither her freedom nor her happiness in this Wonderland. She remains *a foreigner who aspires access to this place of wonders, […] being rejected time and time again until she pays the price: to 'know' what everyone knows, and 'walk' like everyone walks* (Monsalve 2011: 27). A foreigner who desires to be accepted by others being willing to pay any price as she is in desperate need *of going on, despite everything* (Varley 2011b: 37).

How can you live fully in the present when you are haunted by your past? Sometimes your past is like a corpse that feeds on your body. It is as if the corpse is alive and you are dead. It is as if the corpse has stolen your vital breath and laughs at you. Then you have to get rid of the corpse, to remove the past thoughts from your mind. Otherwise this corpse will always be with you in the future. At the same time, it is true that you cannot escape your past as the past is written in your genes, you are connected to your ancestral past, related to your past experiences. Still, it is essential to understand what happened to you in the past and to transcend it. At the end of the day, *you are what you do.*

From the darkness of the past to the light of the future.

No one should live in the house of illusions.

And for this, it is perhaps necessary to start your life over again. This time your life should be that of an *animal tamed* by culture and not of an *animal domesticated* by his past.

Welcome home!

Welcome to the skyscrapers' square crammed with people! Look! The speaker, red in the face, makes his speech! As no one listens to him, he starts to scream and to whisper, to bark and to whistle, to laugh and to cry! In vain! As he keeps on talking, people start talking to each other! No one pays the slightest attention to his words! Why should they? The speaker talks about his personal trauma! No one is interested in the speaker's personal trauma! No one! People start vociferating and laughing! Suddenly the speaker shouts: *Our world is the best of all possible worlds*! The crowd, stunned for a few seconds, burst into wild applause. Then all of them yell: 'We are hungry! We want coins! Coins! Coins!'

Now the square is deserted except for a little girl who, crying silently, waits for her parents to come back for her. When night falls, the little girl goes out like a light. And then a miracle happens. A beautiful angel takes her in his arms and carries her to *the best of all possible worlds*.

Welcome home!

Your home is in your dream where you feel like a child again. Looking curiously at the world, enjoying its wonders, you are excited to discover the Moon's strange shadowy mountains and to write naive poems about the Sun. You travel in your flying house to the edge of the universe. Your life is full of incessant joy. Your soul is free. And you are happy. Sweet sleep, child!

Your home is in a world where people sing in chorus: *let's all dance the crazy cow / the skull does not cry / love serenade / the skull does not cry / does not have a heart.*

Your home is in a world where people pray to: "*A God who counts the minutes and the pence, a desperate God, sensual and grunting like a pig. A pig with wings of gold which tumbles through the world, with exposed belly waiting for caresses, lo, 'tis he, behold our master! Embrace, embrace!*" (Céline 1960: 4-5)

Your home is in a world where while you fight injustice you lose your will to fight, where you are deprived of your freedom, dignity and honour, where your capacity for love is destroyed, where your necessity of belief in beyond is the subject of derision, where you live with pain and sadness, where you cannot overcome the errors produced by innumerable misunderstandings, where your "childish pleasure in telling secrets, asking questions, loving, inoculating doubts, crossing countries, books, theatres" (Barba 2011b: 9) is spoiled.

From ancient times to the present, the human being's place is in the other human being's heart. Love is within you. And you feel alive. Finally, you have returned home.

Welcome home!

The dance of eros-thanatos

"Do we dance? Yes, we do. Or rather, no, we don't dance. We make theatre." (Barba 2008: 2)

The dance of father's death

The story begins with *Once upon a time there was a girl who fell in love with the man of her dreams when she was 17* and ends with *Do you remember the night when your father died?* Love and death are seen as crucial moments in a human life.

With a blank look on her face, immersed in reverie, the Widow of a Basque Officer spins the fragile thread of memories. Going back in time, she recalls her husband's figure. He was so full of life! So powerful! So attractive! An irresistible Don Juan! And, then, one day he got ill. The disease devoured him. Death rose to the surface and caused perplexity, agitation, anger, grief, helplessness. She remembers him leaning on her frail body and the memory hurts her deeply. In a way, it is so true that between love and death, between man's passionate dance of love and his sudden death, there are only a few moments. A leap of thought.

So, *do you remember the night your father died? Do you remember the horses' hooves? The sound of horses' hooves in the narrow street. From the window you see strangers lifting your father out of a carriage and carrying him in their arms. Your mother comes to you and tells you: 'Do not be afraid. Your father is ill. Run to the shop where they sell ice. It is needed to stop the haemorrhage. And then run to the doctor and make him come quickly. Your father is very ill. And then run to the priest's house and inform him. He has to come in haste with the holy sacraments. Hurry up!'* (Barba 2010a: 35-36) And the son runs to save the life of his father which runs out of a body which has ceased to fight. And in the paroxysm of pain, the boy throws the block of ice and the ice shatters. Sometimes you lose and you cannot turn back the pages of your own life. Death is stronger and kneels you down. And even if you get up, you walk your road with an open *wound* inside your soul. There is no bandage to stop the wound bleeding. There is no healing. Death is the only real obstacle man cannot overcome. When the loved one dies it is as if the whole world dies. The sun and the moon die and something deep inside you dies. And then bitter tears flow from your eyes when you look at the sky and hope that the Divinity will mourn your dead in its ancient language and cover his lifeless body in a veil of light. And you hope that his soul will find its way home.

The dance of collective suicide

Or the dance of an apparently mysterious world, a place which seen from a distance makes you desire to enter it and become one of its dwellers, but the moment you arrive, you hear strange murmurs: *I danced with myself last night / My lover is dead,* glimpse limping bodies, burning candles, a red stone, a loaf of bread, blue wings, silhouettes melted in tango embraces, and listen to the sweet charango music or to the terrifying trumpet sounds. Here, you are told: *This is the happiest country in the world, everybody is happy here!* And not, *this is the country where everybody pretends to be happy when in fact everybody ceased to be so* (Culianu 2010: 346). So, in *the happiest country in the world,* the Rock Musician announces: "As we have agreed, not so long ago, it is today that we are going to commit collective suicide". And then the happiest beings of the happiest country in the world drink poison and take farewell. Kisses and hugs. Even the Puppet drinks poison. The scene reaches its climax when the Rock Musician pours poison on the lighted candle and everywhere. There is such a profound sadness in their pretended happiness. It is so depressing to wear the most hideous mask in the world: the mask of happiness! When someone is happy, he does not display his happiness. He is simply happy. To pretend that you feel something, anything, is self-devouring. Why do people wear a mask? Obviously, not for themselves, but for the others. Obviously, because they lack the courage to be sincere, to tell others, for instance, that they are unhappy. Others must know only what they want others to know. So, they torture themselves pretending to be happy for they want others to believe that they are happy. It is so sad. Yes. Unfortunately, that is the way it goes. Anyway, what happens in this scene is a collective death in a collective bed. Irony, irony, and again irony in this dance of death in which the actors seem to scratch on invisible walls: "Shame, shame, shame – that is the history of human beings!" (Nietzsche 2006: 67)

A dance of illusions is performed in a meaningless world where *God has been declared dead*. A world where everyone is allowed to do everything he wants without suffering any punishment. I mean, everything: murder, suicide, hate, betrayal, theft, deception, envy, lies, malice, arrogance, contempt. Endless atrocities. Man wears not only the mask of happiness but also the mask of war. Take off his mask and you will see an evil grimace on his face. So what? So what if man commits criminal acts? So what if there is nothing beyond his predatory thoughts? That is, his *petty thoughts*. Let us not forget that *a petty thought is like a fungus; it creeps and crouches until the whole body is rotten and wilted with little fungi* (Nietzsche 2006: 68). They are the thoughts-fungi man wants desperately to get rid of. Sometimes he succeeds to free himself. Sometimes he ends up in individual or collective suicides.

During the entire scene the characters give the impression of a perfect community. They all limp! They all behave the same! They all pay the price of living in Wonderland! They all drink poison! They all wake up from what seems a dream about death and look into their playing cards to read their future. A weird sentence floats in the air: "Perhaps we are all in Paradise". Yes. A Paradise wherein the *mad cow* is among us.

So, *my sister... let's dance... dance... dance...* in this agonising world that from a distance seems a mysterious, wonderful world.

The dance of empty ritual

The scenic space, remained deserted, begins to drip as when the snow melts it imitates the rain that seeps through the boards of a frozen shack. Or as when a building abandons itself with all its veins and pipes to its own natural desire to collapse (Barba 2012a: IX). And it rains. It rains. It rains. Water droplets slide off the hooks. And I seem to hear Roberta II from *Jack, or The Submission* whispering: *And it rains in my tresses, always raining. My mouth is dripping, my legs are leaking, my bare shoulders are draining, my hair is flowing, everything is flowing, and the stars and the sky* (Ionesco). Everything flows into *a dance of an empty ritual full of potentialities, a dance of theatre-in-freedom, thought-in-life, thought-in-action.* Noah's flood. Dance of purification.

> *The performance refuses to give the illusion of reality attempting to recreate its contractions, dilations and contrasts: its 'dance'* (Barba 1999a: 55).

Sensations-in-words

"Synthetic – that is, very brief. Into a few minutes, into a few words and gestures, we must compress innumerable situations, sensibilities, ideas, sensations, facts, and symbols."

(Marinetti 2009b: 205)

Everybody knows

Everybody knows still no one opens the door to freedom no one wants to be free one is afraid of freedom and runs from it and hides and covers one's eyes with bandages playing cards plastic flowers thin dried strips of animal skin red handkerchiefs nylon bags tablecloths and one sings in chorus and stays in a foreign country and carry on with a life others make one carry on with and troubles oneself a bit not too much only at the beginning and then gets used to eating without being hungry and drinking without being thirsty and oh occasionally one has a small crisis when one remembers what one could have been but one did not dare to be and then it seems that one would wish to be free only that the disease which has crept into every pore of one's being grabbed one's soul oh chronic life mistake guilt remorse suffering as there has been left only a bit of strength to stand on one's feet and to recognise that one was wrong strength not to repeat the same mistakes so to give oneself the chance to make other mistakes the chance to follow one's path to reach one's door and there in front of the door to know that one is the key to the door oh chronic life dead eyes ears nostrils mouth pores one sees no more hears no more smells no more tastes no more touches no more one is dead and one does not even know one is dead

Shut the door!

Oh, your precious travels! What are they for? To intensify your thoughts and feelings and emotions. For a while. And, then? Then, again your old despair. Crisis. Resignation, sadness, sleep, dream. When you want nothing, you are free. To desire nothing to be free. Wisdom is a strange part of your nature. It feeds you. Peace is in you, with you. For a while. Just the time to think a thought. Or two. Perhaps even three. And, then? Out. You go out again. Travel again. And again and again and again. And all of a sudden you feel your travel is the same. Walk in circle. Predictable. Monotonous. Devouring. You travel around the world and feel nothing. No thrill. No excitement. No joy. Still you keep on travelling. To find your true self. You do not find your true self. Perhaps if you increased the number of seconds, hours, days, weeks, months, years of travelling, you would find your true self. Walk. Walk. Walk. Walk in circle. You feel tired. More and more tired. Circle of tiredness. Trapped in your room you open your eyes to shut your eyes. Open to shut. Your eyes shut. Your mouth shut. Waiting for death to knock at your door. No. Not yet. You wish to travel again. One more travel. It is time to pack your bags. Now! All you have to do is to open the door and shut the door. But you do not move. You cannot move. You want to open the window. To see the sky. The blue sky. But you do not move. You cannot move. You know the whole world has its windows open. Why is your window shut? Why? You do not know. Oh, your precious travels! You walked, walked, walked till tiredness put a stop to your walking. Helpless in your circle of darkness. You hear a strange sound. It is the sound of the wings. Do not despair. Soon you will travel again. Prepare yourself for the last travel. The last door. Do not forget to shut the door.

Free-in-Father

To be Free-in-Father. To wonder. Rarely. Free thought. An instant. Not lasting. Silent and burnt inside to grope for freedom. To crave for its endless end. To fly through the tunnel of time. A window opens. A breath of air. Not lasting. Then. Again. *The chronic life.* Repetition. Repeat. Repeat. Repeat. The same life. The same hours. Anguish. Torn inside.

The disease caught you. The limits! You with you. You with others. You with Father. Are you free-in-Father? In? Not far away? Far away? It smells of rain. Freedom. Self-becoming. Freedom plus? Freedom minus? Sensations. Fright causes you angst. Incertitude. Doubt. Despair. *On the heights of despair.* You are not free. Subterfuges. Refuges. Obtuse angles. Mimicries. Then. Then you know. Here. Only here you dream a dream. It is your life in agony. Your life in transition. Your loss. Your helplessness. And you see you do not see. And you know you do not know. Still you hope. There must be a beyond. A never-dying present. Absolute freedom. And then you wait. Nothing happens. Nothing. And then you count. On your fingers. The finger of child. The finger of love. The finger of flight. The finger of fall. The finger of death. Free-in-Father. The mystery of Father. The road of life. War-ant. Justice-ghost. Road-beaten. Litter-glitter. Death-sac. Beyond-sideways. Cold corners. Nani-nana.

Rolling over three times

To run out of time.

You look out of the window. People hurry down the street. It looks like they are running out of time. Looking back nostalgically on your childhood, you put your secret dream in a trinket drawer and hurry down the street. Days, weeks, months, years pass by. One morning you decide to clean out the drawers. And you come across your dream. You stare at it. It is so small, fragile and dusty and all of a sudden in a fit of anger you drop it in the bin and take out the trash. Why didn't your dream help you roll over three times to become the man you have always wanted to be? It was just a worthless dream. Night falls. Rain is on the horizon. And it gets colder. Your eyes hurt. You feel ill. Burning up. In a moment of despair you leave the house and start running to search for your dream in the garbage. The garbage of galaxy. And there you are welcomed by other people's dreams. Lots of sad dreams scattered all over the place. Where is your dream? You are running out of time. So, you ask the first dream you meet in the garbage: 'Have you by any chance seen my dream? It is a dream which stayed too long in a drawer and got ill, it caught a cold, its voice changed and was no longer a dream, I think it turned into an illusion, and the illusion got ill as well, it got a cataract, and I think the illusion turned into a lie, so I got rid of it. But now I feel ill and desperately need my dream. Tell me, have you seen it?'

The invisible: the visible beyond the visible

Something hidden: Invisible to the eye? Invisible inner barriers? Humans turned into shadows? The feeling of being invisible? The logic of paradox? Turning the invisible into the visible or turning the visible into the invisible? A magical hat that makes one invisible? Feeling sad and invisible? The subtle breath of the earth? The black of night? Strange voices? Mysterious silences? Silent steps? Glowing drops of rain? The turquoise wings of angel? The abandoned puppet? The horrifying hooks? The dead flowers? The runs around the coffin? The fragile being who wipes and wipes invisible walls and invisible windows and invisible sails? The ethereal light? The unfathomable depths of love?

A self for sale

You live in two worlds, your inner world and the outer world. And in the outer world you do not say what you really think or express your true feelings because no one does so. You look at others, and do not see their faces, but their masks. You realise that social life is a masquerade, a grotesque carnival. The moment you start wearing a mask, the story goes like this: you live your life according to what others say about you or think about you; the others invade your inner world and your mind becomes preoccupied only with what they say or think about you. So, when you let yourself be inhabited by others it is as if you sell your self to them. Is your self for sale?

A life ring

You work with your body's energy and all of a sudden you see yourself nearly drowning in deep waters; at the last moment you cling on to a life ring; there in the midst of the sea it is you breathing and drifting to unknown realms; feeling totally unbalanced, engrossed in the play of pure energy, you think thoughts you have never thought before;

your soul is joyful, your body has become weightless, and you have endless time to experience with your body the happiness of being changed; your body shivers with pleasure when it is touched by an invisible tender hand that caresses you, sculptures you, colours you, perfumes you, controls you; you feel that someone loves you and takes care of you; it is like a dream that you have and wish you would never wake up from; it is like a process of self-becoming; it is the most fantastic experience of your life.

What about our good old balance?

We make rational efforts to harness the irrational instead of keeping a balance between rational and irrational. We plan our future to avoid the unpredictable instead of embracing our unknowable future. As we are afraid something might change our lives in unexpected ways, we maintain a false balance. At the same time, often, arrogance deludes us into thinking that we are invincible. Being hubristic, we are not shaken in our self-contentment but in moments of crisis. So, our life oscillates between our self-contentment and the *torrid zone of our lack.*

Every day we keep a false balance. Every day we hide our vulnerability and humbleness. It is only in our dreams when we long to share ourselves with the other that we feel strongly imbalanced. It is so because actually, every moment of our life, we crave love. We hope to meet our other half. This meeting never takes place. Never. Why? Mainly because we do not allow ourselves to lose our good old balance.

We cannot move from one stage of existence to the next in the absence of severe crises and profound imbalances. Only if we are capable of (re)gaining our balance every time life brings us to our knees, we move on.

Knock, knock, knock

Knock, knock, knock, you hear knocks at your mind's door. 'Who is it?', you ask. 'The thought', it answers. 'Go away, I don't have time, I'm busy, don't you know?', you yell at it. 'Tomorrow you will be free', the thought murmurs. 'Free? Me? Tomorrow? No way! Are you kidding me? Not tomorrow and not in a hundred years! I have a very busy schedule. I am a very busy person. My time costs money. Money! Money! Money! Go to hell!', you shout angrily. 'Tomorrow you will be free for tomorrow you will be dead', the thought whispers.

In-between

Djianna, my alter-ego, dreams that a fire-breathing dragon menaces her and feeling frightened she pulls on the reins of her little wooden horse. Suddenly an invisible entity opens a space-time fracture and Djianna finds herself inside the belly of the dragon. After a few seconds of bewilderment, she dares to ask him:
   "Please, tell me, is *The Chronic Life* a dream or a reality?"
   "Ssssst! It is only a dream", the dragon whispers.
   "Thank you. I hope I have not disturbed you", Djianna murmurs.
   And she enters another unsettling dream about dew-on-eggs, scorched-steppes, severed-forests, drowned-meadows, oceans-in-plates, weeds-arms, hate-in-caress, devilish-smile, penumbra-umbra, lightning-and-thunder, ghost-flesh, howl-in-hug, blood-stain, old-Thumbelina, virginal-viscera.

At night the hole moves during sleep

You can cope with your emotions but cannot cover the hole inside which grows bigger and bigger; one day, from dawn till dusk, you weave a blanket, arduously; at night you cover your hole with the blanket but the hole moves during sleep and uncovers itself and then you feel cold, agitated and frightened and you know that even if you weave, till your fingers bleed, bigger and bigger blankets, every night, you will have to face the *hole*.

Tenant in one's own body

And I think of that perfidious, illusory illness you fully accept as a real part of your life; it is as if this illness has always been deep inside you; it is as if you were born ill; this happens when you stop fighting and start hating yourself; right at that moment, illness declares itself owner of your body and behaves as an absolute, indisputable controller; first of all, it asks you to pay a rent; then it gives you orders that you must obey otherwise you risk the punishment of death; as time goes on, the orders are getting more and more extreme; moreover, every month it increases the rent and threatens you with eviction; one month you are late paying the rent and illness throws you out; you have only time to pack your soul.

Why don't you hear the cricket chirping?

As you grow old you transform yourself into a perfectly rigid person: rigid thinking, rigid body, rigid expression, rigid behaviour, rigid routine, rigid life. You lost your childish naivety, warm smile, sweet kindness, fragile force, sparkling eyes. And it is amazing that you feel no sadness, no regret for what you lost. You do not ask yourself: 'Why doesn't my soul sing with joy every morning? Why doesn't my heart throb with love? Why don't I hear the cricket chirping? Why don't I run happily in the rain? Why don't I listen to the nature's symphony? Why isn't my thought a living thought? Why don't I miss my true being?' It is all about your states of soul – *states of mind* (Barba 2006: 3).

Face to face

Making reference to the stage illusion, Thomas Mann notices: "Never before except in church had I seen so many people gathered together in a large and stately auditorium; and this theatre with its impressive seating-arrangements and its elevated stage where privileged personages, brilliantly costumed and accompanied by music, went through their dialogues and dances, their songs and routines – certainly all this was in my eyes a temple of pleasure, where men in need of edification gathered in darkness and gazed upward open-mouthed into a realm of brightness and perfection where they beheld their hearts' desire. [...] [The actor] moved so easily within the frame of the musical and dramatic conventions that they seemed, far from restricting him, to release him from the limitations of everyday life. His body seemed informed to the finger-tips with a magic for which we have only the vague and inadequate word 'talent', and which obviously gave him as much pleasure as it did us" (Mann 1955: 29-31). From a distance, the actor/actress appears to be the sincere Romeo or the sweet Juliet, fictional characters endowed with the charming qualities every spectator yearns for. Nonetheless, according to another of Thomas Mann's descriptions, at a close look, the spectator notices the actor's/actress's zits, boils, wrinkles, dark purple eye circles glowing in sweat, the costumes embellished not with emeralds and sapphires but with glittering baubles. When you come right down to it, every dis-enchantment appears to be a re-enchantment on a different level of reality. One of the strongest qualities of a performance is that it makes the spectator believe in its fictitious reality. Engrossed in rehearsals, often dreaming with my eyes open, empathising with the director's vision, many a time I have entered another state of consciousness. The theatre has always been and continues to be a privileged place where the individual lives an extraordinary experience. An experience which, in his ordinary life, he only imagines, longs for, falls asleep with, and dreams about. It is undeniable that the theatre performance is capable of producing powerful experiences making the spectator rediscover himself.

Yes. I feel I am rediscovering myself during rehearsals. Today, I come to realise that the light, in *The Chronic Life*, is used not only as stage lighting but also as character and bridge between fictional worlds. So, here we have the light-character and the light-bridge, the tiniest action as an exemplary action, the meaningful detail, the spoken word that unlocks the doors to the secret chambers of the spectator's mind, the music that is dance, and the dance that is flight. The strips of white light penetrating the darkness intensify the spectator's sensation of unreality. The red light invites him to dance: *Dance with the light*! The metaphysical dimension of the blue light reminds me of Paracelsus' remark: "For heaven is man and man is heaven, and all men are one heaven, and heaven is only one man" (Paracelsus, *Paragranum*). I cannot but think that today as the human being oscillates between faith and absence of faith in Beyond, the actors engage themselves in a perpetual play of opposites, such as *apotheosis and derision*.

It is true that man sometimes feels he is not capable of breaking *the wall of misunderstanding he has himself built*. It is true that the spectator sometimes has the feeling that he does not truly understand a performance. However, at this point, I ask myself: How can I understand fully something that is beyond my power of understanding? I saw hundreds of performances in my life and I dare say that I understood most of them. The moment of understanding was the moment they stopped preoccupying my mind. I realise the complexity and profundity of *The Chronic Life* and I think a performance is not to be understood completely, but to be remembered.

In Barba's *space-river*, the spectator sees the faces of the other spectators opposite him. Thus he has the possibility to notice the other spectators' reactions likely to influence his own reactions. This might be the reason why the actions executed in the *space-river* have to be stunningly attractive so that the other spectators' reactions do not affect his own. The spectator follows the actors' actions, especially those that resonate powerfully in his inner world, not solely with his eyes but with his whole body. Actually *each spectator has to choose and make his own montage, quickly framing first one situation and then the other, or following one of them and ignoring the other, at the same time being aware that the spectator sitting beside him looks in a different direction, choosing according to a different logic and therefore receiving different information* (Barba 2010a: 47). Barba magnificently orchestrates the simultaneous actions reminding me of Marinetti's remarks: "It's stupid to want to explain with logical minuteness everything taking place on the stage, when even in life one never grasps an event entirely, in all its causes and consequences, because reality throbs around us, assaulting us with *bursts of fragments of interconnected events, interlocking together, confused, jumbled up, chaotic.* For example: it's stupid to act out a contest between two persons *always* in an orderly, clear, and logical way, since in daily life we nearly always experience mere *flashes of argument* which have been rendered *ephemeral* by our activities as modern men, passing in a tram, a *café*, a railroad station, so that experiences remain cinematic in our minds like fragmentary dynamic symphonies of gestures, words, lights, and sounds" (Marinetti 2009b: 206). So, the spectator glimpses pebbles of different sizes, shapes and colours in the riverbed of the performance. In the complex process of *making his montage*, he completes it with his own pebbles and thus he creates his own dramaturgy.

Face to face means to see yourself through the other's eyes. *Face to face* also means to see your reflection in a mirror whose surface, slowly liquefying, invites you to step into a *Wonderland*, into a dream: *the spectator dreams; and what do you think he dreams about?; about you, performance; and if he left off dreaming about you, then you, performance, where do you suppose you'd be? nowhere; since you're only a sort of thing in his dream; and you, spectator who dreams, where do you suppose you'd be? nowhere; since you are only a sort of thing of the performance that dreams about you* (Carroll 2016: 40).

The scenic space reminds the playwright-director "of the deck of a ship which tilts and pitches and straightens itself again on a sea which is at times agitated by the wind, at times dead calm, at times disturbed by the sudden turbulence of submarine currents: the actors' actions, their dynamisms, their introverted or extroverted characteristics, their way of using the voice – from a whisper to a scream" (Barba 2010a:

45). The space for *The Chronic Life,* originally designed as a deck of a ship, reminds me of a horseshoe. It is Pegasus, the beautiful winged-horse, sprung from Medusa's blood when Perseus cut off her head, kissing with his horseshoe the hot sand that embraces the sea, that comes to my mind. The space also makes reference to architectural arches, for instance, to the arches of Alhambra palace, causing in the spectator the sensation that the keel of the ship floats in the sky.

The Rumanian Housewife's line, 'Tutto cominciò su una nave arenata nel deserto / All started on a ship stranded in the desert', is cut during rehearsals. However, the feeling that the ship is somehow still present in the scenic space persists even in the final version of the performance when Madonna-Kali, on the roof-deck, swinging the sword like a ship's wheel, gives the impression that she steers the vessel to unexplored, dangerous waters. She seems to look at the dark horizon where the visible and invisible embrace.

"With a bottle of Polish vodka, Eugenio [Barba] christens the set *Medusa's raft.*" (Carreri 2011: 62)

Who could have imagined the horrible destiny of the French frigate *Méduse*? In 1816, on a summer day, it sets off proudly towards Senegal. Unfortunately, it deviates from its route and runs aground on a sandbank off the West African coast on 2 July 1816. However, the story does not end here. 146 men and one woman are abandoned on a hastily constructed raft. The captain and crew aboard the lifeboats intend to tow the raft but, after only a few miles, destiny speaks again, as the raft is turned loose. It floats adrift for 13 days. When the brig *Argus* appears on the horizon, there are no more than 15 survivors. There is still breath in their dying bodies as they hope to be saved.

It is a black page in world history on which unimaginable horrors are written: murder, suicide, cannibalism.

1818-1819: Théodore Géricault evokes the tragedy in his painting *Le Radeau de la Méduse*. This dreadful experience is somehow rooted in *The Chronic Life* as human beings experience the agony of death. Perhaps that is why, at the end of the performance, when the rain falls announcing the end of a world, the spectator feels the futility of life.

Wars. Crimes against humanity. War is like a sharp knife that erases man's belief in a sense of life. A knife scratching off the last shade of honour left in him. Times when the human no longer sees the kind face of another human, but the evil face of a killer.

In the storeroom

"After twenty years in a wooden box
the angel Lolito returned to life
with his turquoise wings
and naive features
which looked like one of the actor's."
(Nagel Rasmussen 2011: 71)

Ice melts and its droplets are like grains of sand pouring through an hourglass to symbolise the passing of time. The sound of trickling water becomes louder when the light fades away. No more words are spoken. No more songs are sung. Only the tears of ice falling inexorably, ruthlessly. Solid matter, gradually, turns into liquid matter till, at the end of the performance, it rains.

Hooks. Are they butchers' hooks? Fishing hooks? The musical instruments, the turquoise wings, the Puppet, the actors themselves seem to be bait hanging on hooks in the storeroom. Can the storeroom also be seen as a place where resuscitation is performed, where the actor is brought back to life by connecting his heart to a power source?

The actors wait, full of expectations, in the storeroom. *They have already prepared a 'store' in the Blue room*: "it was the end wall where musical instruments, props as well as actors, are hung or placed when they are not in action. Some giant hooks make one think of a butcher's shop or a torture chamber" (Nagel Rasmussen 2011: 78). On the one hand, if we are in an abattoir, we may feel horrified by the image of the slaughtered animals, hanging upside down, with their feet tied together. On the other hand, if we are in a *butcher's shop*, we have come to buy *meat,* haven't we? However, what kind of meat? Musical instruments and wings and actors? Are they goods to be bought? To be sold? What are they? Merchandise predestined to be thrown into the world's waste bin? Or do we, stupefied, witness the torture of human beings? "Torture chamber"? Yes. Waiting in seeming stillness for someone, for something, sometimes may be a real torture.

The actor's shining eyes are directed upon the spectators, but aimlessly and somewhat blurred, as though he does not see them

(Mann 1922: 76).

The scenic space reminds me of a room with a wardrobe/storeroom and a bed in the middle. The objects which temporarily inhabit the room are brought in and taken out by the actors. A room in which the bed is a coffin and the storeroom is *an open wardrobe* (Mann 1922: 76), and we, spectators, looking at the Rumanian Housewife see *a creature so lovely that our heart stands still a moment and then in long, deep, quiet throbs resumes its beating; a being with one of her slender arms reaching up to crook a forefinger round one of the hooks in the ceiling of the wardrobe* (Mann 1922: 76), a fragile being who, like Scheherezade, tells us, night after night, a story, the story of our *chronic life, a sad story, without relief, but which rests like a sweet burden upon our heart and makes it beat longer and more blissfully* (Mann 1922: 77). It is as if an angel comes out of the wardrobe and *tells us in a soft voice, while the candle-flame performs its noiseless dance* (Mann 1922: 77), a story about the deathly sleep we have fallen in.

At the same time, the space looks like a monk's cell in which the Young Colombian, praying to find his father, dreaming of Golgotha, relives the destiny of man passed on from father to son. The young boy sets off in search of his father. He does not find his father. He continues to seek him following the path of the Father. *It is all uncertain. Everything must be in the ai r ...* (Mann 1922: 77).

The physical-vocal island

"I have always experienced the voice as a material force which sets things in motion, leads, shapes and calms: an extension of the body. It manifests itself through precise actions provoking an immediate reaction in the person to whom they are directed. The voice is an invisible body which operates in the space." (Barba 2010a: 40)

At times, I close my eyes letting myself be carried along by the musicality of Barba's *sonorous dramaturgy*. The actors' vocal actions transfigure the scenic space in which actor and spectator breathe at the same time. Both of them enter a world of incantation and magical vibration. It is the ineffable world of sounds that soothe, caress, kiss, bite, hit, whip, hurt.

The sounds form words that, *whispering a different story to every spectator* (Barba), do not illustrate reality, but *create reality*. The actors, *masters of the sounds, are capable of getting everything they want through the force of the sound: for instance, love and joy; they are also capable of taming the animals, making the plants grow, bringing the rain or the good weather* (Culianu 1992: 29). Barba comes to conceive his sonorous dramaturgy for *he is obliged to devise an arrangement of vocal actions and peripeteias which can enthral the spectators independently of their comprehension of the words* (Barba 2010a: 40). *His experience makes him discover the existence of the actor's vocal dramaturgy with an autonomous and coherent life of its own which can be detached from the meaning of the words* (Barba 2010a: 40). His vivid sonorous dramaturgy based on pluralities of meanings contributes essentially to the shaping of a dynamic complex dramaturgical universe that aims to ignite the spectator's imagination. In this universe, the almost imperceptible impulse, the tiniest action and the suavest sound are meaning carriers.

The actor rediscovers the sonorous richness through rigorous studies of the sounds made by birds and animals, natural and mechanical sounds, the sounds released by the actor during his improvisations on fundamental themes such as birth, love, death, blindness, madness, sacrifice, suicide, murder, of the sounds which vibrate, of the sound-echo, and of the sound of silence. In this respect, the Odin actors "trained to create a gamut of intonations, sounds and resonators; they reproduced the 'voice' of animals, objects, extra-terrestrial beings; they listened to records with songs from other cultures and imitated them; they repeated the melodic and rhythmic cadences of unknown languages and dialects. They spoke a text as a musical instrument, as the expression of a medium who tells episodes from a supernatural reality" (Barba 2010a: 41).

The director-playwright builds "a constant tension between the sonorous communication and the semantic one by opposing, commenting on and unmasking the meaning of the words" (Barba 2010a: 41). The vocal actions are synchronised with the physical actions as *every vocal action has its roots in the corresponding physical action, and the actor performs it with his whole body, well aware of synchronising the physical impulses with the vocal ones. Without this synchronisation, it is impossible to reach an organic effect* (Barba 2010a: 42).

During his studies of physical-vocal actions, the actor pursues to identify and practice slow and fast, uninterrupted and interrupted, accelerated and decelerated vocal-body rhythms; to exploit efficiently the pauses in the flow of actions; to reach organic effects; to transmit different meanings of words by changing vocal intensities; to produce loud, soft, rustling, strong, weak, short, long, metallic, low-pitched, high-pitched, musical, whispered sounds; to perform the transition from *speech* to *chant* and from *chant* to *speech*; to establish *the equivalence between vocal and physical action*; to analyse the impact of the physical-vocal action on spectators; to make use of different vocal qualities in slow motion and acceleration; to practise different *ways of walking and sitting*; to change the meaning of the action according to different scenic situations and relationships; to metamorphose the action according to the scenic space and props; to personalise the physical and vocal exercises; to use mnemonic exercises to develop creativity; to follow a crescendo / decrescendo pattern, etc..

Barba's 'real actions' *are the actor's actions that follow a dynamic logic* which is independent from the narrative meaning and which often refers to the capacity to display the 'equivalent of the energy' – quality of tensions, dynamic design, effort, acceleration, manipulation, etc. (Barba 2010a: 26). During the process of metamorphosing his actions, the actor reveals unspoken thoughts, intentions, hesitations, certainties, decisions and doubts many times emphasised by the forcefulness or softness with which he performs the action. In order to acquire the skills required to execute *real actions*, it is necessary, for him, to transcend his body-voice limits he may not even be aware of. As *to know does not mean to become aware of your freedom, but of your own limits: it means to find out what is already pre-established or sometimes to find out what is already in you* (Culianu 1992: 30).

The actor's body is his instrument of expression that he trains "to be like a Stradivarius, with the stimulus coming either from his inner self or from others" (Lindh 2010: 31).

Sometimes, during rehearsals, I have had the feeling that the actors produce distinctive vocal sounds with a power capable of breaking walls, modulate their voices to create *circles of rough air, circles of thin air, invisible bells* whose sizes they constantly change. Using different vocal registers, they give the impression that with their voices they build deep tunnels, sculpt fabulous animals, devise odd objects, or establish unpredictable relationships with the space. I remember some of their *real actions* have a strong *organic effect* on me: blowing out a candle, praying for inner-peace, writing a love letter to the dead lover, riding a wooden horse to the garden of childhood, playing blind man's buff.

Other times, I have felt totally immersed in the sonorous universe created by the director "with the aim of establishing an emotional dialogue with *each* spectator" (Barba 2010a: 42) and in which "Every action is in reality a reaction: to a thought, a necessity, a sound or another person's action" (Carreri 2007: 87). A peculiar universe in which I could hear the ice melting; the rain of the metallic coins falling; the crack of the gun; the dull sound of the stone thrown with violence; the creepy sound of running footsteps; the abrupt knocks on the chest, on the floor, on the door; the heart beating like a drum; the clattering of pans; the groan of the coffin lid; the clink of the spoon hit against the plate; the sizzle of fire; the riffle-shuffle of the playing cards; the sounds of the musical instruments that stir emotions like joy and sorrow; the beautiful, unearthly sound of love. Yes: "the force of the sound has no limits" (Culianu 1992: 31). It is as if the actors who speak in Danish, Norwegian, Spanish, English, Chechen, Basque and Romanian incarnate "a sonorous dream" (Culianu 1992: 32). It is a dream in which every sound has the force of an action: *Odin Teatret's language – the means of expression the actors use – is a language of action in space* (Bredsdorff 2004: 40).

The time to be humble

"Theatre activity has a double effect: on the person who carries it out and on the person for whom the work is intended – the spectator. The introduction of the exercises has made it possible to define and delve deeper into the zone of 'the actor's work with himself'. The exercises are not aimed at muscular development, but at mental and somatic concentration on a modest but complicated task that sometimes may be paradoxical. The necessity for precision and repetition determines a specific way of thinking with the entire body by means of a concatenation and simultaneity of tension, contrast and dynamic immobility. It is learning *to be* as an actor, to grow roots through a scenic presence, but it is also a process of individualisation and personal growth. It is no coincidence that the term 'exercise' is to be found in all paths of psychic, mental, or spiritual transcendence which make use of somatic processes: a particular way of breathing, fixing one's gaze, moving, dancing, or halting the flow of thought." (Barba 2002d: 24-25)

The actor is a person who continuously trains to surpass his personal limits. Therefore, to make theatre, for him, involves a process of self-knowledge and self-becoming. In gentle solitude, in his "secret garden which is the place where he can cultivate his dreams and his professional nostalgia" (Carreri 2007: 113), he reinvents stories and reinvents himself. A fruitful *meditation*. A mental exercise. A personal time.

The time of self-growth. The time of creative freedom. The time to experiment. The time for mistakes, misunderstandings and paradoxes. The time of the 'body in movement' *considered and accepted as a 'language' that cannot be translated but that is perhaps best able to express profound images* (Schino 2009: 72-73).

The time when he sets out a journey inside his *mind-body* to his self, "for the self alone embraces the ego and the non-ego, the infernal regions, the viscera, the *imagines et lares*, and the heavens" (Jung 1971: 159). A voyage of exploration, discovery and self-discovery.

The time in which he aspires to become a *master of the sound,* of the Beckettian voices, being aware that "To discover one's own voice means to discover one's own interior universe, one's own soul" (Nagel Rasmussen 2018: 283).

The time when through mental exercises he aims to identify and cultivate that *part in him,* which I call the *observer,* that is necessary for lucid analysis, critique and self-critique. The time when he develops his intelligence, capacity of listening, attention, observing, self-observing and distancing himself from the character he creates.

The time of identification. The time of alienation. The time of the character conceived, in multiple layers, by the actor rooted in his *scenic self.* The time when he goes through different stages during the process of knowing his *self* and knowing the outer world. The time when it is essential for him to maintain a balance between reflection and feeling, intelligence and emotion, to let himself be guided by his *living thought* as *reflection, understanding and judgment are also affective reactions, that is emotions* (Barba 2012: 89). The time when the actor becomes aware that to transmit emotional intensity, he has to be a *body-in-life* and not a ventriloquist-body: "Laughter, eroticism and fear have for centuries been the elementary ingredients of theatre spectacles, both of the many coarse and vulgar ones, as well as of the few that are spiritually sharp. Today it seems that the theatre can do without elementary ingredients, like an idealised body deprived of its genitalia. Like a body censored by the intelligence or the intelligentsia. It seems that the task to awaken Angelanimal once again – our shadow with wings but also with four legs – has been delegated to other types of performance. The theatre has become purified. It has become a disinfected niche, intelligent and cultivated, even when it exhibits naked bodies and simulates copulation. I wonder: why, today, is theatre only intelligent? Why only cultured? Is a brain consisting of only the cortex still a brain or is it merely a monstrosity?" (Barba 2006: 3-4)

The time to immerse into his fictional worlds. To dig deeper into his *self* that "includes not only the conscious, but also the unconscious psyche" (Jung 1928: 188), to listen to his inner voice.

The time *of the Procrustean bed,* when *the actor's body sometimes appears to be chopped, sometimes stretched to fit the scenic form,* is the time when he explores different ways of manifesting his creative freedom within the rigorous scenic forms.

The time of revelation. The time to create his enigmatic presence. The time of thoughts incarnated in words, chants and actions, *living signs*. The time to dance. To share. To be humble. And then: "We dance as if on glowing coals. [...] *As if* we had wings; *as if* mighty roots sank deep into the earth under our feet; *as if* our 'I' was another; *as if* we were free. But humbly, because for us this dance must have the humility of a craft, and is barely more than the exercise of the *as if*" (Barba 2008: 2).

The time to recall his childhood. To think back to his roots: *the fear of trapping the sacred animal in the darkness of the well, a certain box of buttons, a night that lasts a lifetime, a glass-fronted locker which Captain Rossi opened with a doll's key, an umbilical cord severed by one's own hands, a father who had no time to grow old and suffer because of an estranged son, the family flaw, a knot of impulses, a solitary fortune-seeking* (Barba 2010a: 4-6). The time to remember and to dream.

The time of solitude and reflection. Thoughts on his *relative lack of adaptation which turns out to his advantage as it enables him to follow his own yearnings far from the beaten path* (Jung 1971: 109).

The time for feeling at home, as *a laboratory is first and foremost a 'home', an abode inhabited not by 'actors' but by a group of individuals who have their own stories, identities and personalities, and who work in a group, emphasising that what marks out a theatre laboratory from all other theatres is training called an island of freedom for the actor* (Schino 2009: 224-227).

The time for the awakening of the mind.

The time of the burning passions.

The time, for me, to paraphrase from George Orwell: *Training is a horrible, exhausting struggle. One would never undertake such a thing if one were not driven on by some demon whom one can neither resist nor understand. For all one knows that demon is simply the same instinct that makes a baby squall for attention. And yet it is also true that one cannot train unless one constantly struggles to efface one's own personality* (Orwell 2005: 10).

The training of self-becoming

"The dance of oppositions is danced in the body before being danced with the body." (Barba-D'Urso 2000: 42)

For the Odin actor, training is essential in creating his organic dramaturgy as *the living roots of the performance are not a literary text, a story to be told or Eugenio Barba's intentions as director, but are a particular quality of the actors' physical and vocal actions: presence, scenic bios, organic effect, seductive persuasion, body-in-life* (Barba 2010a: 25). Training, the director remarks, *does not teach how to act, how to be clever, it does not prepare one for creation; training is a process of self-definition, a process of self-discipline which manifests itself indissolubly through physical reactions. What counts is the individual's justification for the work because this personal justification decides the meaning of the training. This inner necessity determines the quality of the energy which allows work without a pause, without noticing tiredness, continuing although exhausted and even then going forward without surrendering* (Barba 1999b: 79). Barba operates a distinction between *daily and extra-daily body technique* "designating the actor's extra-daily technique as a particular use of the body with the aim of achieving a scenic presence"; at the same time, the director identifies "principles which are always to be found at the foundation of the performers' scenic presence in all traditions and genres. Such 'recurring principles' are alteration of balance, emphasis on opposing tensions within the body, equivalence, consistent inconsistency, omission, and also sub-score" (Barba 2010a: 30).

In the first years of training, Barba *blends together the most diverse influences, the impressions which for him had been the most fertile: Asian theatre, the experiments of the European Theatre Reform, personal experience from his stay in Poland and with Grotowski* (Barba 1999b: 82). Gradually, the actors personalise their exercises, but it is definitely "not the exercises in themselves that are decisive, but one's personal attitude, that inner necessity which incites and motivates the choice of one's profession, justifying it on an emotional level and with a logic that will not allow itself to be trapped by words" (Barba 1999b: 81). Through assiduous research, the director discovers *the value of personal images for engaging the voice in order to attain one's individual sound universe* (Barba 1999b: 83) *as well as the value of vocal action, of the voice as a prolongation of the body which, through space, hits, touches, caresses, encircles* (Barba 1999b: 83). *Training, which can only be individual* (Barba 1999b: 82), represents the foundation of the actor's process of self-discipline and self-becoming and contributes decisively to Barba's dramaturgy creation.

The actors train every day

Today Roberta Carreri creates a sequence of actions metamorphosing her white serviettes into dust cloths, handkerchiefs, boxing gloves and bread crumbs. In her working process, the actress *does not follow a linear logic, but an evocative logic which advances in leaps* (Carreri 2007: 92). Then she works together with Jan Ferslev on a scene in which they improvise different types of hugs. In another scene, Ferslev breathes life into his musical instrument and manipulates it in such a way that it reacts like a living being to the actor's impulses. The musical instrument, the same as the voice, is a prolongation of the actor's body. Thus the instruments that *in their own way live and think* (Barba 2012a: IX) participate in the creation of a scene. And not only the instruments but also the costumes: Tage Larsen plays with his blue leather jacket in order to create contrasting images. And not only the instruments and the costumes but also the props: Iben Nagel Rasmussen creates a fight dance in which she handles a sword with one hand while with a red handkerchief held in the other hand, sometimes intensifies the dance of the sword and sometimes abates it; Julia Varley, with surgical precision, cuts the playing cards while Kai Bredholt runs like the wind through the space.

The actors work in "collective solitude" (Carreri 2007: 113). It is extraordinary how cohabiting in the same space they do not disturb each other. The songs they rehearse many times are neither an accompaniment nor an illustration of their actions but a means through which they expand their search for expression. At the same time, during their explorations, the actors fight against predictability and mannerism. There is such a difference between a mechanical interpretation and an organic interpretation, the latter being the result of a long process in which director and actor work in a symbiotic relationship often taking into account the spectator's possible reactions.

After watching the actors' training day after day, I have fully realised that it is essential for the actor to be constantly open to new creative ideas to inspire him and make him reflect on; it is crucial to give himself the chance to change himself both as actor and human being; it is necessary to continuously work with himself; it is vital to train every day as lifelong training is the actor's true journey to his self.

Epistle to Augusto Omolú

I still feel the energy of your soul. I still see your body arching in full fight with the powers of nature, the book breathing in your hands, your elegant suit, black shoes, exquisite handkerchief. You are both animus and anima, Othello and Desdemona, force and fragility. Completely absorbed in watching your dance in *Orô de Otelo*, I wonder how it is possible to dance with so much passion and tenderness, vigour and precision.

You tell me: an actor accomplishes his assiduous work with all his heart. As time goes by, an actor does not lose his will and strength to attain his artistic goals, to make his dreams come true. As time goes by, an actor who loves his work becomes more and more charismatic fascinating the spectators with his impressive virtuosity.

Wilderness and kindness in your dialogue between you as Othello and you as Desdemona, between jealousy and love, between misunderstanding and understanding, between imbalance and balance. It is Othello's destiny to be caught up in the web of Iago's poisonous lies. When Desdemona dies, Othello dies. Love dies. Alas, *the serpent* is always the winner.

I will never forget your love for dance.

Augusto Omolú, for me, you will always be Othello.

An affectionate hug
Diana

To speak about freedom is always a must

"We must be sand, not oil, in the machinery of the world."
(Barba 2002c: 8)

To have the strength, resistance and unbroken will to pursue his quest for the meaning of art and life, to openly express his opinions and discuss important ethical dilemmas, to speak out against social, cultural, political inertia and injustice, to give himself the freedom to say things in his own unique way, to bring novelty into his artistic domain are some of the most important personality traits of an artist *who does not allow himself be assimilated and succeed in 'not' sharing the values which seem imposed by the circumstances and the spirit of the times* (Barba 2010a: 13).

It is true that a work of art transcends its historical moment. But it is also true that often the artist who is considered a political threat is the victim of an oppressive regime. It is a historical fact that different forms of cultural censorship were applied in the ex-communist countries. Sometimes even aesthetics was used as a means of minimising the impact of an artist's work. More than that, the history provides us information about the dramatic destinies of those artists who, opposing authoritarian governments, suffered persecution. Many of them were exiled or buried in oblivion. One way or another, an artist speaks about the human being's necessity to be free. We need our freedom to express ourselves. Therefore we must never forget that to speak about freedom is always a must.

It is impossible "to imagine an artist today applying for a grant from the Ministry of Culture to research the Truth through theatre. Or the director of a theatre school writing in its programme: 'here we teach acting with the aim of creating a New Human Being.' Or perhaps a director who demands from his actors to know how to dance because it mirrors the harmony of the celestial spheres" (Barba 2010a: 18).

Freedom and truth are *qualities* an artist gravitates towards. We may even say that "All art forms are based on the individual's relationship to the truth" (Flaszen 2010: 95). Often an artist searches for historical, political, social, existential truths which constitute sources of inspiration for his work which sometimes reveals his *spirit of justice*. At the same time, his propensity to find the truth of a given historical period is likely to enhance his capacity of visualising the future, his *prophetic vision*. George Orwell's vision of a totalitarian system in his novel *1984* is eloquent in this regard. An artist may live for a very long time in his ivory tower, *far from the madding crowd*, in order to reflect upon society's mentalities and changes. However, both his inner world and the outer world are subjects of investigation and artistic transfiguration.

Any society functions on a set of rules of behaviour respected by its members. Each time a society progresses, its members' patterns of behaviour change. Referring to progress, Thomas Mann asserts: "There was progress, [...] without doubt there was progress, from Pithecanthropus Erectus to Newton and Shakespeare had been a long and definitely upward path. But as with the rest of Nature, so too in the world of men everything was always present at the same time, every condition of culture and morality, everything from the earliest to the latest, from the silliest to the wisest, from the most primitive, sodden, barbaric to the highest and most delicately evolved – all this continued to exist side by side in the world, yes, often indeed the finest became tired of itself and infatuated with the primitive and sank drunkenly into barbarism" (Mann 1955: 294). Primitivism, pragmatism, digitalism coexist today. The actual individual, at the same time primitive and pragmatic, breathes in a digital world. Unfortunately, manifesting his pragmatism, uninterruptedly, within society, he, at a certain point, comes to treat the others solely as goods, that is as *objects*. We may even say that throughout history there has always occurred a transfer of identity from human to object. So, the value of an individual is measured by the objects he has in his possession. It is evident that the individual's attitude towards the others suffers radical changes during the adolescence-adulthood transition. It is only a leap of thought from his daydream to his down-to-earth interests. Pursuing concrete objectives, he becomes fully aware that in order to build himself a successful career he himself must change. Seeing the others as *objects which possess objects,* the individual tortures his mind to find out exactly how to be the way the others want him to be in order to gain the objects he craves. When the individual treats the other as an object, he himself turns into an object and in turn is treated by the others as an object. This kind of living, solely in the outer and for the outer, makes the individual believe that he is *someone* because he has *something*. Caught in the chains of *to have* he forgets about his freedom *to be*.

Where does the individual's desire to be constantly in fashion come from? Perhaps from his fear that others might treat him as being out of fashion, obsolete, dusty, useless. Obviously, it is a perfidious trap as, after all, "You must be asocial to realise what is possible for *you*" (Barba-D'Urso 2000: 220). I think each of us, as each of us is unique, should try to find his personal voice. To untiringly cry out: *I am in fashion! I know the books in fashion! The movies in fashion! The performances in fashion! I know everything which is in fashion!* is a limited way of expressing oneself. Is it also conventional thinking that reduces his capacity of accomplishing himself as a unique human being? M. Scott Peck's answer to this question, in his famous book *The Road Less Travelled and Beyond,* is *yes* (Peck 1997). To conform exclusively to trends and fashions, for instance, cultural trends and fashions, may affect his personal growth and cause a split between what he really is and what he must pretend to be. In fashion. Pretending to be what he is not, striving to build himself only a public image, he consciously and voluntarily accepts endless compromises. He wants so much to be in fashion that he specialises to become specialist in being in fashion. I think he should always pay attention both to his inner and social life in a continuous attempt to keep them in balance as "inasmuch as individuation is a quite indispensable psychological requirement, it is possible to infer from this estimation of the superior force of the collective, what extremely careful attention is demanded by this tender plant, individuality, if it is not to be completely smothered by the collective" (Jung 1928: 161).

Sometimes an artist criticises the follies of society. Other times, he reveals the dark side of the human nature. And other times he speaks about love or about the joy of simply being alive. In a grotto or a tower, the artist isolates himself to totally dedicate himself to his work. And, there, in his grotto or tower, he feels free.

"However, many think about the theatre in two dimensions, as if what mattered was only aesthetics, ideological tendencies, artistic results, or different techniques. The *ethos* is the dimension of depth, the measure of the relationship between one's individual history and History." (Barba 2002b: 184)

In Antiquity the actors were slaves and in the Renaissance they were treated as *vagabonds, beggars or the scraps of society*. Today we live in a world in which the actors are admired, even idolised and the institutionalised and independent theatres coexist amicably. But we also live in a world in which, according to Eugenio Barba, for the people who fight for their rights, theatre is a stringent necessity and a powerful means through which they express their dreams, ideals, experiences and protests. *The Third Theatre, a concrete manifestation, in various parts of the world, of a thirst for dignity and values* (Barba 2010b: 21), refers to the *theatres which live on the margin*: "Theatres on the margin are not marginal theatres. They try to defend a margin, an empty space which lets itself be filled with nostalgia and personal necessities. They fight against the invading aesthetics, ideologies, techniques, poetics, fashions. They want an empty ritual, not usurped by doctrines" (Barba 2012a: 166). The theatre of *rebellion and dissidence* emphasises the role of theatre in the struggle against any form of oppression and aims to make people change society. In this respect, the work in theatre generates individual and collective identity and transformation and has a liberating effect on its participants.

For Barba, there is no frontier between his personal and professional life. His work is nurtured by his passion for theatre and by his freedom to express his thoughts and ideas.

> To make theatre involves a continuous struggle with oneself to be oneself.
> To make theatre involves to expand the horizon of one's knowledge.
> To make theatre involves discipline and self-discipline.

To make theatre requires *not to let oneself be one with his own mask, social definition, not to identify with his role* (Barba 2010b: 14).

To make theatre involves one's freedom of thought and action.

The miracle of longevity

"To act, in the theatre, means to intervene in time and space in order to change and to be changed."
(Barba 1993a: 162)

What might longevity mean in the case of an artist? Undoubtedly, longevity implies resistance in hard times, permanent research, continuous personal growth, uninterrupted search for his *authentic self*. At the same time, longevity refers to his capacity of never forgetting his dreams, never turning his back to his origins, never anchoring his roots in an apparently safe ground, never adapting to the norms, and never cutting the thread *linked to the child in him who bewitches him and compels him to be out of place and out of time* (Barba 1999b: 19). Even though longevity means also biological ageing, it is evident that an artist's life and professional experiences often contribute majorly towards enhancing his fascinating personality. In other words, at a certain age, he emanates *wolfness*. What is *wolfness*? The meaning of the word is to be found in Eugenio Barba's proposal for an improvisation: "On a carpet, a wolf is born three times. The first birth is the biological one. The second is the transition which places the anonymous person among those who have a name. Through a rite of passage lasting eleven days and eleven nights, you become a wolf. The third birth happens in old age. It occurs when the others recognise in you the authentic wolf, when you emanate wolfness" (Barba 2010a: 136). Undeniably Barba's charismatic presence makes the others feel fully alive and at the same time eager to see his extraordinary performances, to participate in his spectacular miracles.

For an artist, *to become a legend* involves a process of assiduous and incessant work, a lifetime act of generosity. Dwelling in his fictional worlds and dreams, he has to remain solidly anchored in the *terra firma* of the contemporary historical realities he lives in. In-between these two worlds, fictional and real, the artist works to become immortal through his creations. His ephemeral body turns into ashes but his works turn into diamonds that never die.

Eugenio Barba accepts the challenge of change. When he is not allowed to enter Poland, being declared *persona non grata*, and consequently cannot continue his research with Jerzy Grotowski, he founds Odin Teatret in Oslo, Norway, on October 1, 1964, changing his life radically. Two years later, when he receives a proposal for his theatre to be provided with a space and a minimal subsidy, he moves to Holstebro, Denmark, and if, in the first years, he is preoccupied with "ensuring the material and professional survival of a group of very young actors, who were amateurs and autodidacts of differing nationalities and languages" (Barba 1999a: 9), in the following years, he develops his personal research achieving remarkable results. Like Pablo Picasso, Barba goes through his own *Blue Period, Rose Period, Cubism* and *Surrealism*. During the Odin Teatret's first year in Holstebro, Barba creates the Nordisk Teater-laboratorium, an organisation that studies the actor in performance, researches training and rehearsal methodologies, studies performance forms in various cultures, the latter culminating in Barba's founding of the International School of Theatre Anthropology in 1969 (Watson 1993: 3). *Beginning with ISTA, the recurrent principles of actors' and dancers' technique are the basis for his research both theoretical and practical, comparative and pedagogic, on the behaviour of human being in an organised performance situation* (Barba 2012a: 99). The Odin Teatret and Theatrum Mundi performances and the revolutionary approach of dramaturgy are also a significant part of Barba's tremendous work.

"I have often spoken of theatre as of a haemophiliac body losing blood as it collides with reality, as a ghetto of freedom, a floating island, a fortress filled with oxygen, a canoe rowing against the current and yet remaining on the same spot like the third bank of a river; of theatre as a house with two doors, one for entering and one for flight; of theatre as the people of an empty ritual; of theatre as a ship of stone which can take us on a journey through the experiences of the individual and of history; of theatre as a wall which obliges us to stand on tiptoe to see beyond it; of theatre as barter, potlatch, waste, emigration. These are metaphors which suggest a craft which is valid only if it transcends itself and searches for its value by striving to liberate itself from its function merely as performance." (Barba-D'Urso 2000: 330)

In more than 55 years of existence, Odin Teatret has become a *tradition-in-life*. Actors, directors, students, from all over the world, strongly attracted by the director's and his actors' *professional excellence* (Barba 2012a: 22), group ethics, discipline and self-discipline, are willing to work under their guidance. In this respect, Odin Teatret is a meeting place between theatre practitioners of different nationalities and languages emphasising the fact that "Multiculturalism, in the country of the theatre, is not an emergency. It is something obvious which belongs to its act of birth" (Barba 2005: 2).

On the director's *ship of stone*, the actors bring to life characters which tell the spectators timeless stories about life and death. Leaving behind the waters explored by the theatre ancestors, Barba sails his ship to unexplored regions. He wishes *to fight for something very precise, to sink his roots in the sky, in a country of values without frontiers, where the truths would be the fruit of a conflict and personal conquest* (Barba 2012a: 16).

All the participants in *Odin Week* 2009 are fascinated by Eugenio Barba's magnetic personality and unequalled capacity of transmitting knowledge. I remember like it was yesterday what he told us during his seminars.

Here are a few observations Barba made in one of his seminars:

A complex web of interrelated actions which *suggest* and not *affirm* is preferable to a succession of events based on the deductive logic.

The actor's vocal and physical actions aim to reflect the *quality of any living organism* which oscillates continuously between *order* and *disorder*.

Through his training, *a process of self-becoming*, the actor pursues three major objectives: to apply the principle of *opposition* and to make use of *paradoxical thinking* and *simultaneous actions*.

The actor's dramaturgy is a *sensorial – spiritualised dramaturgy* or a *meta-carnal* dramaturgy whose golden rule is *synchronicity* according to which the actor's body and voice manifest concomitantly.

While I was listening to Eugenio Barba, scenes from *Inside the Skeleton of the Whale* came to mind. The actors' unearthly presences, their ethereal movements and divine singing, the exemplary scenic space of great simplicity are still vivid in my mind.

Barba's *floating island, island of freedom, which is just a grain of sand in the whirl of History and does not change the world, yet sacred because it changes us* (Barba 2003: 3) is an island of research, training and work, an island of asceticism which "always characterizes the apprenticeship in *excellence*, artistic or sportive, spiritual or competitive. Self-discipline accompanies the efforts of each individual to go beyond his limits. The training of the actor is the initiation into a profession in which resistance, in its multiple meanings, is a fundamental condition: physical and psychical control; persistence in adversity, in failure, in the fruitless winter periods; avoiding self-indulgence and rejecting obvious solutions; stubbornness in the face of obstacles; perseverance in extracting the difficult from the difficult; tenacity in order not to adapt to circumstances" (Barba 2012a: 49). It is also an island of dramaturgy. Eugenio Barba's dramaturgy addresses the contemporary spectator, that is the actual individual overwhelmed by the huge amount of information, subject to a variety of stimuli, responding to the quick changes in the external environments, reacting to actions which occur at the same time. The individual, in himself, is an entity who changes from one second to another. These might be a few reasons why Barba conceives his dramaturgy on multiple levels of organisation as a web of simultaneous vocal and physical actions and allusive narrations. The evocative narrations reverberate powerfully in the secret rooms of the spectator's inner house. And so the spectator keeps alive the performance and his reactions to the performance in his memory. Thus his memories become part of *the longevity of the artist and his work*.

If we understand that we do not understand anything and thus, admitting our ignorance, we strive to understand why we do not understand, perhaps we succeed in avoiding the discursiveness of our mind which repeats the same thoughts and desires again and again. There is always room, in ourselves, for discovery, for expanding our knowledge horizon.

And then longevity is to never give up on our dreams.

Azure

"I was fifteen years old when I went to the theatre for the first time. My mother took me to see *Cyrano de Bergerac*. The hero was played by Gino Cervi, a very popular Italian actor. But it was neither he nor the other actors who impressed me, nor the story which they were telling, which I followed with interest but without amazement. It was a horse. A real horse. He appeared pulling a carriage, according to the most reasonable rules of scenic realism. But his presence suddenly exploded all the dimensions which until then had reigned on that stage. Because of this sudden interference from another world, the uniform veil of the stage seemed torn before my eyes." (Barba 2004a: 47)

Today, at the beginning of rehearsal, Eugenio Barba asks the actors to sing a song and, all of a sudden, he starts to sing and dance! It is such a joy to listen to his singing and to watch his dancing! Today is a day full of surprises! The director works on the actors' vocal and physical actions, deconstructs their lines into words, words into syllables, syllables into vowels and consonants, analyses the meanings of the lines in detail, exploits the pauses between the sounds and the micro-actions. He is so full of energy that I cannot take my eyes off him! Suddenly, the rehearsal is interrupted by a group of children who are paying a visit to the theatre. Eugenio Barba takes the children by the hand and together they run round in circles, run and laugh, and unexpectedly the lights go out and then, in that very moment, the director and the children begin screaming and shaking with laughter and clapping their hands and then the children joyfully leave the Red room to continue their miraculous journey through the theatre. The director continues working on the precision of the steps, the expressiveness in the body movements and postures, the rigour of the actions. Inch by inch, he devises a perfect dance of the actions. While watching him, suddenly a thought comes to my mind: the director asks the actors to perform the actions that he himself has already experienced with his body-mind. It is true, for Barba, there is no difference between theory and practice!

Today has been a beautiful day!

Often, during rehearsals, with a pen which he takes from a pocket of his colourful shirt, he records his thoughts, ideas, observations in his notebook. Thinking with his whole body, he refines the tiniest scenic action guiding the actors in the process of creating their scores. At times, his actions are so unpredictable that they take me by surprise. He has such a passion for theatre, such a hunger for new artistic experiences, he is so alive, so energetic! Eugenio Barba himself is the performance he works at.

The rehearsal is the time when the director identifies with the actors' actions and at the same time distances from them; a time when traversing the stage with feline steps he whispers secrets in the actors' ears; a time of tremendous work and revelation; a time when the director foresees the future of the performance; the time of his vision of dramaturgy. For me, it is a time when I feel no longer that I am a small wheel in a social mechanism, that I have a certain age or profession or social function, that I belong to a certain country or language; a time when I am simply living a unique experience which addresses my human nature; a magic time when I feel myself alive and happy even though I know that this time will never return.

The rehearsals conducted by Eugenio Barba, a magnificent personality and a powerful charismatic director, are fantastic artistic adventures which nurturing my mind and my heart make me feel the same elation which I feel when I look out of my little window and see the azure sky.

Bibliography

Artaud, Antonin. 1958. *The Theater and Its Double*, translated from the French by Mary Caroline Richards, New York: Grove Press

Barba, Eugenio. 1985a. *The Gospel according to Oxyrhincus*, play, Holstebro: Odin Teatret

Barba, Eugenio. 1985b. *Lions, Mad in the Desert* in programme for *Oxyrhyncus Evangeliet*, Holstebro: Odin Teatret

Barba, Eugenio. 1993a. *The Paper Canoe: A Guide to Theatre Anthropology*, translated by Richard Fowler, London and New York: Routledge

Barba, Eugenio. 1993b. Lecture at Quebec University, Montreal, 30.11.1993

Barba, Eugenio. 1995. Seminar for Actors at Theatre du Lierre, 1995

Barba, Eugenio. 1996a. *Un amuleto fatto di memoria. Il significato degli esercizi nella drammaturgia dell'attore*, in Marco De Marinis (editor), *Teatro Eurasiano n. 3: Drammaturgia dell'attore*, Porretta Terme: I Quaderni del Battello Ebbro

Barba, Eugenio. 1996b. *Cultural Identity and Professional Identity* in Kirsten Hastrup (editor), *The Performers' Village: Times, Techniques and Theories at ISTA*, translations by Judith Barba and Leo Sykes, Graasten: Drama

Barba, Eugenio. 1997. Lecture at Facultad de Humanidades y Artes Rosario, 09.12.1997

Barba, Eugenio. 1998. Conference at Arena del Sole, Bologna, 1998

Barba, Eugenio. 1999a. *Land of Ashes and Diamonds. My Apprenticeship in Poland* followed by *26 Letters from Jerzy Grotowski to Eugenio Barba*, translated from the Italian by Judy Barba, Aberystwyth: Black Mountain Press

Barba, Eugenio. 1999b. *Theatre: Solitude, Craft, Revolt*, translated from the Italian by Judy Barba, Aberystwyth: Black Mountain Press

Barba, Eugenio. 2000a. *Sonning Prize Acceptance Speech*, Copenhagen University, 19 April 2000

Barba, Eugenio. 2000b. *Tacit Knowledge: Heritage and Waste*, translation by Judy Barba, in John Andreasen and Annelis Kuhlmann (editors), *Odin Teatret 2000* Aarhus: Aarhus University Press

Barba, Eugenio. 2001. Encuentro con Eugenio Barba "Delfines Terrestres", Teatro El Cuenco, Córdoba, 2001

Barba, Eugenio. 2002a. *Arar el cielo: Diálogos latinoamericanos*, La Habana: Fondo Editorial Casa de las Américas

Barba, Eugenio. 2002b. *The House with Two Doors*, translated from Spanish by Susana Epstein, in Ian Watson, *Negotiating cultures. Eugenio Barba and the intercultural debate*, Manchester and New York: Manchester University Press

Barba, Eugenio. 2002c. *In the Guts of the Monster*, Speech of thanks on the occasion of the Honorary Doctorate bestowed on Eugenio Barba by ISA, Instituto Superior de Artes in Havana on 6 February 2002, translated by Judy Barba, at https://odinteatret.dk/media/3797/2002-havana-univ-en-discurso-honoris-causa-in-the-guts-of-the-monster.pdf, accessed on 5.07.2019

Barba, Eugenio. 2002d. *The Essence of Theatre*, in TDR/The Drama Review, Vol. 46, No. 3, 2002, pp. 12-30

Barba, Eugenio. 2003. *The House of the Origins and the Return*, Speech on the occasion of conferring the title of Doctor honoris causa by the University of Warsaw, 28.05.2003, at https://odinteatret.dk/media/3798/2003-warsawa-univ-en-discurso-the-house-of-the-origins-and-the-return.pdf, accessed on 10.07.2019

Barba, Eugenio. 2004a. *A mis espectadores: Notas de 40 años de espectáculos*, translated by Rina Skeel, César Brie, Raúl Jaiza, Lluís Masgrau, Arturo Rodriguez Peixoto, Gijón: Oris Teatro

Barba, Eugenio. 2004b. *Children of Silence: Reflections on Forty Years of Odin Teatret*, translated from Italian by Judy Barba, in programme for *Andersen's Dream*, Holstebro: Odin Teatret

Barba, Eugenio. 2005. *The Paradox of the Sea*, Speech on the occasion of conferring the title of Doctor honoris causa by the University of Plymouth 27.10.2005, translated by Judy Barba, at https://odinteatret.dk/media/3799/2005-plymouth-univ-en-discurso-honoris-causa-the-paradox-of-the-sea.pdf, accessed on 10.07.2019

Barba, Eugenio. 2006. *Angelanimal: Lost Techniques for the Spectator*,

Speech of thanks on the occasion of the Honorary Doctorate bestowed on Eugenio Barba by Hong Kong Academy for Performing Arts on 7 July 2006, translated by Judy Barba, at https://odinteatret.dk/media/3800/2006-hong-kong-univ-en-discurso-honoris-causa-angelanimal.pdf, accessed on 13.07.2019

Barba, Eugenio. 2008. *In Praise of Fire*, Speech of thanks on the occasion of the Honorary Doctorate bestowed on Eugenio Barba by the National University of the Arts (IUNA) of Buenos Aires, on 5 December 2008, translated by Judy Barba, at https://odinteatret.dk/media/3801/2008-buenos-aires-univ-en-discurso-honoris-causa-in-praise-of-fire.pdf, accessed on 3.07.2019

Barba, Eugenio. 2010a. *On Directing and Dramaturgy: Burning the House*, translated by Judy Barba, London and New York: Routledge

Barba, Eugenio. 2010b. *Prediche dal giardino*, Mondaino: L'arboreto Edizioni

Barba, Eugenio. 2011a. *Incomprehensibility and Hope* in programme for *The Chronic Life*, translated from Italian by Judy Barba, Holstebro: Odin Teatret

Barba, Eugenio. 2011b. *The First Day* in programme for *The Chronic Life*, Holstebro: Odin Teatret

Barba, Eugenio. 2012a. *La Conquista della differenza: Trentanove paesaggi teatrali*, Presentazione di Ferdinando Taviani, Roma: Bulzoni Editore

Barba, Eugenio. 2012b. *Fama e fame*, Speech of thanks on the occasion of the Honorary Doctorate bestowed on Eugenio Barba by Babeș-Bolyai University of Cluj-Napoca on 2 November 2012

Barba, Eugenio. 2012c. Conference at the Writers' Union of Romania, Cluj Branch, 3 November 2012

Barba, Eugenio, and Tony D'Urso. 2000. *Viaggi con Odin Teatret / Voyages with Odin Teatret*, translation by Judy Barba, Milano: Ubulibri

Barba, Eugenio, and Nando Taviani. 2004. *Seven Meetings between Andersen and Scheherezade*, translated from Italian by Judy Barba in programme for *Andersen's Dream*, Holstebro: Odin Teatret

Barba, Eugenio, and Nicola Savarese. 2006. *A Dictionary of Theatre Anthropology: The Secret Art of the Performer*, second edition, translated by Richard Fowler, London and New York: Routledge

Biner, Pierre. 1972. *The Living Theatre*, New York: Horizon Press

Brecht, Bertolt. 1978. *Brecht on Theatre: The Development of an Aesthetic*, translated by John Willett, London: Methuen

Bredholt, Kai. 2004. *Many Layers of Paper with Glue in between*, translated from Danish by Anne Savage, in programme for *Andersen's Dream*, Holstebro: Odin Teatret

Bredholt, Kai. 2011. *Donna Vera*, translated from Danish by Erika Sanchez and Judy Barba, in programme for *The Chronic Life*, Holstebro: Odin Teatret

Bredsdorff, Thomas. 2004. *A Dream Come True* in programme for *Andersen's Dream*, Holstebro: Odin Teatret

Bredsdorff, Thomas. 2011. *The Chronic Theatre*, translated from Danish by John Irons, in programme for *The Chronic Life*, Holstebro: Odin Teatret

Büchner, Georg. 2014. *Woyzeck*, translated by Gregory Motton, with an introduction by Kenneth McLeish, London: Nick Hern Books, published: 9 October 2014, accessed 5 August 2019

Carreri, Roberta. 2002. *There Are Rivers and There Are Volcanoes*, English translation by Tom Kingdon, in programme for *Salt*, Holstebro: Odin Teatret

Carreri, Roberta. 2007. *Tracce — Training e storia di un'attrice dell'Odin Teatret*, edizione a cura di Francesca Romana Rietti, fotografie di *Orme sulla neve* di Guendalina Ravazzoni, Prefazione in forma di lettera di Eugenio Barba, Milano: Il principe costante Edizioni

Carreri, Roberta. 2011. *Our Chronic Life*, translated from Italian by Elena Masoero and Kemal Ibrahim, in programme for *The Chronic Life*, Holstebro: Odin Teatret

Carroll, Lewis. 2016. *Through the Looking-Glass and What Alice Found There*, edited by Brinda Bose, Delhi: Book Land Publishing Co.

Céline, Louis-Ferdinand. 1960. *Journey to the End of the Night*, translated from the French by John H.P. Marks, New York: New Directions Publishing Corporation

Chaikin, Joe. 1973. *La présence de l'acteur* in *Travail Théâtral*, cahier trimestriel, n° 12, 1973, Lausanne: L'Âge d'Homme

Chevalier, Jean and Alain Gheerbrant. 1995. *Dicţionar de simboluri:*

Mituri, vise, obiceiuri, gesturi, forme, figuri, culori, numere, vol. 2, E-O, București: Artemis

Craig, Edward Gordon. 1957. *On the Art of the Theatre*, London: Heinemann

Culianu, Ioan Petru. 1992. *Pergamentul diafan*, traducere de Dan Petrescu, București: Nemira

Culianu, Ioan Petru. 2010. *Tozgrec*, ediție îngrijită și traduceri de Tereza Culianu-Petrescu, Iași: Polirom

De Marinis, Marco. 1987. *Dramaturgy of the Spectator*, translated by Paul Dwyer, The Drama Review: TDR, Vol. 31, No. 2, pp. 100-114, published by The MIT Press

Flaszen, Ludwik. 2010. *Grotowski & Company*, translated by Andrzej Wojtasik with Paul Allain, edited and with an introduction by Paul Allain, with the editorial assistance of Monika Blige, and with a tribute by Eugenio Barba, Holstebro – Malta – Wrocław: Icarus Publishing Enterprise

Gilbert, Daniel. 2006. *Stumbling on Happiness*, New York: Vintage eBooks at https://www.academia.edu/35150248/Stumbling_on_Happiness, accessed on 21.07.2019

Ionesco, Eugène. 1958. *The Bald Soprano* in *The Bald Soprano and Other Plays*, translated by Donald M. Allen, New York: Grove Press

Ionesco, Eugène. 1958. *Jack, or The Submission* in *The Bald Soprano and Other Plays*, translated by Donald M. Allen, New York: Grove Press

Jung, Carl Gustav. 1928. *Two Essays on Analytical Psychology*, translated by H.G. and C.F. Baynes, London: Baillière, Tindall and Cox

Jung, Carl Gustav. 1971. *Spirit in Man, Art, and Literature* in *Complete Works*, vol. 15, translated in English by R.F.C. Hull, Princeton University Press

Khayyám, Omar. 1909. *Rubáiyát*, rendered into English verse by Edward Fitzgerald, New York, London: Hodder and Stoughton

Ledger, Adam J. 2012. *Odin Teatret: Theatre in a New Century*, Basingstoke: Palgrave Macmillan

Lindh, Ingemar. 2010. *Stepping Stones*, translated by Benno Plassmann and Marlene Schranz with the assistance of Magdalena Pietruska, edited and introduced by Frank Camilleri, Holstebro – Malta – Wrocław: Icarus Publishing Enterprise

Mann, Thomas. 1955. *Confessions of Felix Krull, Confidence Man. Memoirs Part I*, translated from the German by Denver Lindley, London: Secker & Warburg

Mann, Thomas. 1922. *The Wardrobe* in *Stories of Three Decades*, London: Martin Secker & Warburg Ltd at https://archive.org/details/in.ernet.dli.2015.124817 published on 2012-09-05, accessed on 17.07.2019

Mark in *King James Bible*, at https://www.kingjamesbibleonline.org/Mark-Chapter-7/ accessed on 13.07.2019

Marinetti, Filippo Tommaso. 2009a. *Let's Murder the Moonlight!* in *Futurism: An Anthology*, edited by Lawrence Rainey, Christine Poggi, Laura Wittman, New Haven & London: Yale University Press

Marinetti, Filippo Tommaso, Emilio Settimelli, and Bruno Corra. 2009b. *The Futurist Synthetic Theater* in *Futurism: An Anthology*, edited by Lawrence Rainey, Christine Poggi, Laura Wittman, New Haven & London: Yale University Press

Mei Lan Fang. 1986. *My Life on the Stage* to which is added *The Enchanter from the Pear Garden* by S.M. Eisenstein, International School of Theatre Anthropology, stampato a Roma dalla Tipo-Graf, October 29th 1986

Monsalve, Sofia. 2011. *What My Father Left Me*, translated from Spanish by Stephano Regueros Savvides Garcia, in programme for *The Chronic Life*, Holstebro: Odin Teatret

Nagel Rasmussen, Iben. 1984. *Marriage with God*, Holstebro: Odin Teatret

Nagel Rasmussen, Iben. 2000. *Fragments of an Actor's Diary*, translated from Danish by Julia Varley and Nigel Stewart, in John Andreasen and Annelis Kuhlmann (editors), *Odin Teatret 2000*, Aarhus: Aarhus University Press

Nagel Rasmussen, Iben. 2011. *Meaning in Madness*, translated from Danish by Judy Barba, in programme for *The Chronic Life*, Holstebro: Odin Teatret

Nagel Rasmussen, Iben. 2018. *The Blind Horse: Dialogues with Eugenio Barba and Other Writings*, A.P. La Selva editor, Ghent: Adriana La Selva

Nietzsche, Friedrich. 2006. *Thus Spoke Zarathustra: A Book for All and

None, translated by Adrian Del Caro, edited by Adrian Del Caro and Robert B. Pippin, Cambridge: Cambridge University Press

Odin Teatret Film & Odin Teatret Archives, *Physical Training at Odin Teatret,* Work demonstration at Odin Teatret (1972), production: Odin Teatret Film, version restored in 2012 in collaboration with Centro Teatro Ateneo of La Sapienza University of Rome

Odin Teatret Film & Odin Teatret Archives, *Vocal Training at Odin Teatret,* Work demonstration at Odin Teatret (1972), production: Odin Teatret Film, version restored in 2012 in collaboration with Centro Teatro Ateneo of La Sapienza University of Rome

Odin Teatret Film & CTLS Film Archives, *Training at Grotowski's Teatr-Laboratorium in Wrocław,* Plastic and Physical Training (1972), Odin Teatret Film in collaboration with Servizi Sperimentali RAI

Odin Teatret Film & CTLS Film Archives, *Dressed in White,* A chapter from the story of a town crier (1974-1976), produced by Odin Teatret Film

Odin Teatret Film & CTLS Film Archives, *Theatre Meets Ritual, Odin Teatret in Amazonia* (1976), production Kurare & Odin Teatret Film

Odin Teatret Film & CTLS Film Archives, *Ascent to the Sea,* Odin Teatret's street production *Anabasis* (1977-84), production Odin Teatret Film

Odin Teatret Film & CTLS Film Archives, *In the Beginning Was the Idea,* based on the performance by Odin Teatret *The Gospel according to Oxyrhyncus* (1985-1987), production Odin Teatret Film

Odin Teatret Film & CTLS Film Archives, *The Echo of Silence,* a work demonstration by Julia Varley, Odin Teatret (1992), production Claudio Coloberti for Odin Teatret Film

Odin Teatret Film & CTLS Film Archives, *The Dead Brother,* a work demonstration by Julia Varley, Odin Teatret (1992), production Claudio Coloberti for Odin Teatret Film

Odin Teatret Film & CTLS Film Archives, *Doña Musica's Butterflies,* a performance by Odin Teatret (1997), production Lars Amfred Film/Jan Rusz for Odin Teatret Film

Odin Teatret Film & CTLS Film Archives, *The Whispering Winds,* work demonstration by Odin Teatret's Ensemble (1997), produced by Claudio Coloberti for Odin Teatret Film supported by the Institute of

Polish Culture at Warsaw University and the European Commission of the Leonardo da Vinci Programme

Odin Teatret Film & CTLS Film Archives, *The Conquest of Difference: Half a Century of Theatre*, a film by Erik Exe Christoffersen, production Odin Teatret Film, Holstebro, 2011-2012

Orwell, George. 2005. *Why I Write*, New York: Penguin Books

Panigrahi, Sanjukta. 1996. *Five Meetings* in Kirsten Hastrup (editor), *The Performers' Village: Times, Techniques and Theories at ISTA*, translations by Judith Barba and Leo Sykes, Graasten: Drama

Peck, M. Scott. 1998. *The Road Less Traveled and Beyond: Spiritual Growth in an Age of Anxiety*, New York: Simon & Schuster

Pinter, Harold. 1971. *The Caretaker*, London: Methuen & Co. Ltd.

Renan, Ernest. 1897. *Life of Jesus*, translated and with an introduction by William G. Hutchison, London: Walter Scott LTD

Ruffini, Franco. 2010. *L'attore che vola: Boxe, acrobazia, scienza della scena*, Roma: Bulzoni Editore

Sartre, Jean-Paul. 1989. *No Exit and Three Other Plays,* translated from the French by S. Gilbert, New York: Vintage International

Savarese, Nicola. 2010. *Eurasian Theatre: Drama and Performance Between East and West from Classical Antiquity to the Present*, translated from the Italian by Richard Fowler, updated version revised and edited by Vicki Ann Cremona, Holstebro – Malta – Wrocław: Icarus Publishing Enterprise

Schino, Mirella. 2009. *Alchemists of the Stage: Theatre Laboratories in Europe*, translated from Italian and French by Paul Warrington, Holstebro – Malta – Wrocław: Icarus Publishing Enterprise

Shakespeare, William. 2005. *Macbeth*, fully annotated, with an Introduction, by Burton Raffel (general editor), with an essay by Harold Bloom, New Haven and London: Yale University Press

Taviani, Ferdinando. 2011. *The Black Indies of Odin Teatret*, translated from Italian by Judy Barba, in programme for *The Chronic Life*, Holstebro: Odin Teatret

Turner, Victor. 1988. *The Anthropology of Performance,* Preface by Richard Schechner, New York: PAJ Publications

Varley, Julia. 1997. *Wind in the West: A character's novel*, Holstebro: Odin Teatrets Forlag

Varley, Julia. 2011a. *Notes from an Odin Actress: Stones of Water,* London and New York: Routledge

Varley, Julia. 2011b. *The Birth of Nikita: Protest and Waste,* in programme for *The Chronic Life,* Holstebro: Odin Teatret

Vian, Boris. 2003. *Foam of the Daze,* translated and with an introduction by Brian Harper, Tam Tam Books

Watson, Ian. 1993. *Towards a Third Theatre: Eugenio Barba and the Odin Teatret,* with a foreword by Richard Schechner, London and New York: Routledge

Wethal, Torgeir. 2018. *Mirrors Damaged by Damp and Rust: Andersen's Dream, 2004* in Iben Nagel Rasmussen, *The Blind Horse: Dialogues with Eugenio Barba and Other Writings,* A.P. La Selva editor, Ghent: Adriana La Selva

www.ingramcontent.com/pod-product-compliance
Lightning Source LLC
LaVergne TN
LVHW041335080426
835512LV00006B/462